What the E

Insights for Sales ~~...~~

"Fred brings the ability to ask questions the audience was asking themselves while listening. This allows listeners to gain insights they want, not just more messaging. I have had the opportunity to be a guest on the *Sales Game Changers Podcast*, but unlike many other podcasts I appear on, I am also a listener. Looking to make use of this book!"

> —*Tibor Shanto, Chief Prospecting Officer at Renbor Sales Solutions Inc.*

"Sales gurus love to talk, and it can be challenging to boil their insights into small, digestible nuggets. But that's what Fred Diamond does with this book. It's brilliant because it condenses thousands of pages of transcripts and delivers only the absolute best, most perceptive, and most actionable ideas. Elmore Leonard said, 'When you write, try to leave out all the parts readers skip.' Somehow, Fred did it. That's what makes *Insights for Sales Game Changers* such valuable reading for sales professionals."

> —*Mike Schmidtmann, Trans4mers LLC*

"The same creativity and smarts that birthed the Institute for Excellence In Sales can be found in the pages of this book. Fred Diamond has done a masterful job of capturing and presenting insights from dozens of sales game changers and distilling them into a useful guide that professional sellers can use to continue their progress toward excellence."

> —*Matt McDarby, President of United Sales Resources and three-time published author of sales leadership books*

"The book that's more powerful than a search engine. View *Sales Game Changers* as your instant source to uncover real answers to real questions. You don't read this book, you apply this book!"

> —*Mark Hunter, "The Sales Hunter" and author of A Mind for Sales*

"Fred's book is an invaluable resource for sales managers and top sales professionals who aspire to 'best practice' sales management and who aspire to VP of sales and Chief Revenue Officer positions."

> —*John Asher, CEO of Asher Strategies*

"Fred has brilliantly curated insights from hundreds of podcast guests, including myself three times, into a game-changing book for sales professionals around the globe."

> —*Jennifer Fisher, MBA, Senior Vice President of WorldStrides and host of* The Life You Love *podcast*

"From in-person trainings to the *Sales Game Changers Podcast* to webinars delivered around the world, Fred has accumulated a wealth of knowledge on sales encapsulated in this book. It is a must-read, whether you are a tenured rep or breaking into the sales industry."

—*Darrell W. Gehrt, Senior Vice President of Sales at Event Cloud Solutions*

"*Insights for Sales Game Changers* is a must-read for sales leaders at all stages of their careers."

—*Gary R. Milwit, Executive Director, Learning and Organizational Development,*
The J. G. Wentworth Company®

"Fred Diamond has done the impossible. His new book, which addresses the most important topics facing salespeople and sales leaders, is a gem that incorporates the best ideas, strategies, tactics, and mindsets of the greatest sales experts of this generation. Read this book today!"

—*Dave Kurlan, Founder and CEO of Objective Management Group Inc.*

"Most sales authors (me included) tend to write about [their] One Gospel of Sales, perhaps because their audience likes easy solutions. The truth, of course, is more nuanced. Perhaps because his career has focused on results, Fred Diamond is naturally eclectic and pragmatic. It makes sense that he would write a collection of wisdom from multiple sources, and the results speak well for themselves."

—*Charles H. Green, author of* Trust-based Selling, *co-author of*
The Trusted Advisor *and* The Trusted Advisor Fieldbook

"Fred Diamond has interviewed over 500 of the best thought leaders in sales. Then he condensed all of that wisdom into *Insights for Sales Game Changers*. This is a must-read for any sales professional looking to improve their game!"

—*Andy Miller, CEO, www.BigSwiftKick.com*

"If you are looking to raise your sales game, the *Sales Game Changers Podcast*—and thus this book—is a phenomenal resource packed with innovative ideas, proven strategies, and unparalleled experience from a wide array of fantastic guests. If you are looking to not only sell more, but become more, I highly recommend this book!"

—*Alan Stein Jr., author of* Raise Your Game *and* Sustain Your Game

Insights for Sales Game Changers: Lessons from the Most Important Sales Leaders on the Planet

BY FRED DIAMOND

This book is dedicated to all of the sales game changers, like you, who are committed to taking their sales careers, and their lives, to the next level.

Table of Contents

Letter to the Reader 7

Foreword 11

What You'll Find in This Book 13

Prologue 21

Chapter 1: Leading Customers and Salespeople to Success 23

Chapter 2: Account Planning: Your Future Self Will Thank You
for Being Strategic 39

Chapter 3: Every Sales Interaction Is a Conversation that Grows
a Relationship 49

Chapter 4: Urgency: You Need Compelling Reasons to Act 59

Chapter 5: Creativity: Yes, Anyone Can Be Creative . . . with Practice 63

Chapter 6: Succeeding in Sales with Emotional Intelligence 69

Photos with *Sales Game Changers Podcast* Guests 75

Chapter 7: Understanding What Empathy Is and What It's Not 77

Chapter 8: Listening and Questioning: Practical and Powerful Tips
and Strategies 85

Chapter 9: Getting Mentored and Coached Are Essential for
Career Success 97

Chapter 10: An Optimal Sales Mindset Is a Must 105

Chapter 11: Sales Prospecting Is Easier When You Apply These Ideas 113

Chapter 12: Top Sales Professionals Have Indispensable Relationships
That Pay Off for Decades 123

Chapter 13: The Top Reps Prepare and Here's Why 131

Chapter 14: Knowing How to Speak Your Value Proposition Is a Must 137

Chapter 15: Bringing it All Together Like a Professional 147

Acknowledgements 149

Index 151

Letter to the Reader

Thank you for taking time to read *Insights for Sales Game Changers: Lessons from the Most Important Sales Leaders on the Planet*. I'm impressed by every sales professional who picks up a book to read, attends any Institute for Excellence in Sales (IES) live program, or listens to my *Sales Game Changers Podcast*. You're working on taking your career to the next level, and I applaud you for that.

I'm not going to let you down. You'll learn a lot by reading this book. You'll meet experienced and successful sales leaders. You'll be inspired by them and will get some new ideas on how to become a more successful sales professional. That's my commitment to you.

Even though a large part of my career was spent on the marketing side—channel marketing at Apple Computer, industry marketing at Compaq Computer, and product marketing at the large software developer Compuware—I've always been most impressed by the sales side. When I went to work for myself as an outsourced marketing leader, my motto was "Marketing that doesn't lead to revenue reward is a huge waste of time and money."

That motto resonated with a lot of people. As a consultant, I had over 100 clients who depended on me to develop and implement marketing programs that would drive sales. It eventually led to the creation of the Institute for Excellence in Sales, which has become the foremost center for sales excellence in the industry.

And it led to the creation of the *Sales Game Changers Podcast*, which has had over one million interactions, and to the global growth of the IES.

As I like to say, it's about sales.

My first job after college was as a wet-behind-the ears market analyst and tech writer for McGraw-Hill Publishing. I started out writing reports on telecom vendors and trends. Eventually, I moved to a publication focused on information security and quickly became an expert on data encryption devices, bank data security, and access control. I had no idea what I was writing about, but my reports were being well received by both our customers and executives across the globe.

I made it a point to understand as much as I could about the entire organization and each job's functions. I was curious about the process—from deciding which products to develop to customer service. But the corporate sales group interested me most—the pros who sold most of our publications to large IT organizations. Although I did not truly learn the customer's buying process until I went to Apple Computer, I was impressed by these sales leaders, including their manner on the phone and how they talked to customers.

After I worked a few years at McGraw-Hill, Apple Computer's Federal Sales Division recruited me. I was thrilled to work for the best company in the world at that time. But I was in for a rude awakening when I showed up for work. Almost everyone at Apple at the time was super smart and the sales organization was filled with some of the top sales professionals in the industry. They came from companies such as Xerox, Oracle, and IBM. The big boys.

My day of reckoning came when one of the reps scheduled me to present to thirty technical customers. I received the slide deck that morning from corporate and glanced over it a few times beforehand. As I started the presentation, I realized quickly I had no idea what I was talking about. I couldn't answer the first question that came from a customer. Remember when Sarah Palin told Katie Couric that she would get back to her? She got that from me.

Luckily, one of our top system engineers was in attendance and was able to quickly bail me out. At that moment, I said I was never going to be unprepared again, which is something we discuss in Chapter 13. There is no excuse for not being prepared.

Although my first job was in managing our field service partners, my boss made it a mandate that I attend as many sales meetings as I could. In the beginning, I would take a seat off to the side and take lots of notes. I soon realized that the top salespeople were good at finding resources, and when they saw me attending their meetings, they began to see me as a resource who was interested in their success. They took me on sales calls, which showed the customer that Apple had a lot of resources committed to their success. I soaked in what the salespeople told me and made sure that I asked them the right questions.

I eventually moved into channel marketing with Apple and then industry marketing at Compaq Computer. My last real corporate marketing job was with a large software company in Detroit called Compuware. They were known for mainframe software and wanted to move into client/server software. Since most of their sales were to IBM data centers, direct sales was critical to the company's success. I learned how important direct sales was to the company there and applied a lot of what I learned to the companies I started consulting to in the new millennium.

When I decided to make the IES my full-time job, I quickly noticed that my pipeline was slim, so I needed to come up with a solution. I loved listening to podcasts and realized there were none devoted to interviewing sales leaders at companies, so I grabbed onto that platform. Since sales leaders were my target, featuring them on a podcast gave me a chance to meet with them and eventually invite them to join the IES as a member or sponsor, which many of them did.

Starting and hosting my podcast helped me share profitable sales insights with sales professionals looking to grow their careers. The ideas we've gleaned from the more than 500 guests have helped salespeople around the globe discover how to do their jobs better, how to service their customers, and how to be more effective at sales.

I'm glad that you're taking your career growth into action by reading my book. Good for you!

Fred Diamond
Vienna, Virginia
May 2022

Foreword

As you begin to read this book, I hope you will take a moment to reflect on something that will enhance your reading enjoyment: This book can change your life! I know that sounds like hyperbole, but it isn't. Allow me to explain.

First, let me give you a bit of background about myself so as to hopefully give more credence to what I want to share about Fred Diamond and this compendium of sales wisdom. I have been a student of the science of sales for more than twenty-five years. I have led field research in a number of inquiries about sales best practices and have published two business best sellers. Among the things I have learned, there is one often disheartening fact: Too many average professionals are showered with accolades, too many authors of sales books have nothing new to add, and too many texts are not worth the time. Nothing could be further from the case with the gem you are holding in your hands or examining on your screen.

I have known Fred Diamond from the day he founded the Institute for Excellence in Sales. I can say without reservation that he has contributed to our profession far in excess of his notoriety. He believes in sales as a truly admirable profession and has dedicated himself to helping salespeople and sales leaders achieve the full measure of their capability. And he has done so with an understanding that the customers, clients, stakeholders, and sellers in any company will all recognize much greater value when sellers can execute with excellence and sales leaders can establish clarity of mission and task.

Over the past few years, Fred has interviewed hundreds of recognized sales leaders representing many different companies and industries. From this enormous database, Fred curated a set of insights that he has presented in this outstanding guidebook to sales excellence. Further, he has managed to present this extraordinary content in an easy-to-absorb and engaging fashion. This is one of those rare compilations that can serve as both interesting and informative reading cover-to-cover, and as a valuable reference to which any sales professional can return again and again as their career unfolds.

I am confident that however you choose to read this book, you will be amazed at the rewards you garner. Reading these chapters is like having the best of the best advising in every area that sellers and their leaders need to master.

I wish you good reading and great success!

Tom Snyder
Founder and Managing Partner
Funnel Clarity Inc.

What You'll Find in This Book

It's been a life-changing experience interviewing over 500 sales leaders around the globe for the *Sales Game Changers Podcast*. Every day, sales professionals like you download the show or read the transcript to learn ways to take your sales career to the next level. The insights we gained from our sales leader guests have been inspiring, instructional, and constructive.

In this book, we identified the thirty words that have been uttered the most on the podcast and then found some of the most salient and informative examples our guests shared.

Some of the comments have stuck with me as mantras. Perhaps the most impactful was when Gary Milwit advised us to treat everyone we speak with as if they're the most important person in the world. I've shared it with salespeople to use when prospecting, pitching, and interviewing.

We narrowed down the list to the top fourteen words or topics so that you could get through the book in an hour and use it as a trusted and inspirational resource.

Those topics are:

1. Leadership
2. Strategic Account Growth
3. Conversations
4. Creating Urgency
5. Creativity
6. Emotional Intelligence
7. Empathy
8. Listening and Questioning
9. Mentoring and Coaching
10. Mindset

11. Prospecting

12. Relationships

13. Research and Preparation

14. Value

We provide exceptional insights in the book from some of the world's top sales minds and practitioners.

Leadership, Chapter One

There are two ways to look at sales leadership: leading your team and leading your customers. On the podcast, we speak frequently about both, and have uncovered ideas on how to optimize both. Since we only interview top sales leaders, we've been able to uncover how they think and their processes for growing both entities.

Strategic Account Planning, Chapter Two

When you talk about growing your accounts, sales leaders recommend asking what the customer needs now and moving forward. It's becoming standard for prospects and customers to get information on the internet and social networks before they consider calling you. Sales professionals need to bring more value than they've ever had to bring before. We call this bringing "extreme value."

In a dramatic shift over the last couple of years, sales professionals found they needed to think hard about both what the customer is challenged with and what the customer's *customer* is challenged with. If you're not helping them solve their business problems or the business problems that they're looking to solve for *their* customers, you are providing no value to them.

In thinking about account planning, development, and strategy, sales professionals need to specify how they will help their customers achieve the goals that they need to achieve. You need to look at the account and demonstrate strategic thinking that will help them solve their problems well before they even ask you to do so.

For effective account planning to happen, you need to bring in other team members, perhaps people on the tech side. Marketing can help take a deep look into where the customer's industry is going and contribute there.

Look into the future to understand where their customers might be going, so you show them you are with them for the long run. Effective account planning involves showing that you're teamed with your customer and are committed to whatever they need to be successful in achieving their business goals.

Conversations, Chapter Three

Many sales leaders believe that sales is about having the right conversations at the right time and, of course, with the right person or partners who influence activities with your customers and prospects. Are you having as many conversations go well as you need to? If not, how can they improve?

You can ask several questions to determine if you're having effective, meaningful conversations:

- Are you preparing yourself for each conversation?
- Do you take notes?
- Do you listen effectively?
- Are you giving your customers the right opportunity to tell you what you need to hear?

On the *Sales Game Changers Podcast*, expert guests have discussed how to have impactful conversations to move your business forward. Some leaders have said that the sales process is about getting from conversation to conversation. The conversations that you have with your customers need to demonstrate how committed you are to their mission and that you are listening to them.

Creating Urgency, Chapter Four

Customers are under bigger challenges than they've ever been under before, because the challenges of providing value for their customers are deep. If there's no urgency in bringing them solutions, then you're going to struggle with getting the customer to move forward when you need them to do so. They'll move on from you and find the solution from someone else.

The cliché "What have you done for me lately?" applies in sales every day. You need to be assertive in bringing these solutions to your customer and you cannot waste time waiting to bring value.

Your company needs you to have that sense of urgency. The tenure of the average underperforming sales leader is less than two years. You do not have a lot of time to prove yourself, especially if you are not bringing solutions quickly to the customer.

Creativity, Chapter Five

Your customers will be approached by dozens, if not more, sales professionals, so they're going to hear a lot of the same pitches. If you're in a competitive situation where the customer has asked for several vendors to present solutions, you're all going to seem similar after a while.

How can you appear different? How can you come up with new and interesting ways to show the customer that you are providing value to them? Creativity is a huge asset of elite sales professionals and is a critical characteristic of top salespeople. As the opportunities you have in front of customers decreases, and as the customer continues this trend of being in control of the relationship, creativity and differentiation are paramount.

Read this chapter to find unique ways to connect and interact with your clients, so they remember you in a good way.

Emotional Intelligence, Chapter Six

Colleen Stanley, author of two leading books on this topic, helped our community understand the ability for sales professionals to develop and grow what some people refer to as "soft skills," such as empathy and accountability.

They are necessary skills—not just soft skills. They're important in a world that's dramatically changed over the last couple of years and because we've become much more conscious and aware of what people are going through. Customers expect more from us. Read this chapter to see how to develop this vital ability.

Empathy, Chapter Seven

Empathy isn't "feeling sorry" for someone. It's a powerful and proven way to communicate with people. It includes the ability to understand where your customer is at this moment, internalizing the emotional state of the person you're working with and then showing them that you're present, and being honest about where they are.

Sales professionals struggle with this, so that's why we included strategies on it in this book. As a matter of fact, we had a classic moment on the *Sales Game Changers Podcast* where somebody asked one of our guests, "What should I be doing because I'm suffering from empathy fatigue?" The guest, a VP of sales, very smartly said, "If you, as a sales professional, are suffering from empathy fatigue, take a break. Go away for the weekend, go to the mountains, go to the beach. Because that is the essence of successful sales and relationships. It is the ability to understand where your customer is or the person that you're talking to. Not from your perspective, but from their perspective."

It's become a bigger challenge virtually because we only see people on the screen and cannot touch them. But empathy is a critical ability for sales professionals to understand. Once again, it's critical that sales professionals empathize from the perspective of the customer, not from their own perspective.

Listening and Questioning, Chapter Eight

I frequently ask my guests, "What is it about you that makes you a unique and special sales leader?" They say things like, "You have two ears and one mouth, you should use them in that order," or they reference the 66 percent solution (two ears to one mouth). Time and time again I hear, "I am a great listener."

I started asking them, "Tell us something specific that makes you a great listener." One thing we like to say is that a sales call will be a great sales call if the customer is doing 90 percent of the talking. We've heard stats, such as the better sales professionals speak 40 percent of the time on a sales call.

You cannot listen from the perspective of wanting to talk. You must put yourself in the customer's position so that you can understand how you could bring them value. So many people look like they're listening, but in essence, they're just waiting for their opportunity to talk. The top sales leaders that we've dealt with have all figured out that you must make it about the customer, not about you.

You must go in with that plan that the customer must do most of the talking for you to succeed. Customers will always find more value in what they say versus what you say. That's how it goes in conversation, and this chapter gives you strategies and ideas to do it better.

We like to say, "WAIT. Why am I talking?"

Mentoring and Coaching, Chapter Nine

Mentoring and coaching aren't the same. When you're asking for someone to be a mentor, you're asking for career advice. How can I get into leadership? How can I become a more established leader in this marketplace? How do I grow relationships with senior customers in the marketplace? You're usually asking someone who's already done that, someone who's had the expertise in building out that skill or path in your career.

Coaching requires more of a commitment. You must want to be coached. As a matter of fact, we work with a lot of coaches at the Institute for Excellence in Sales, and a lot of them say they'll turn people down because they don't believe the person wants to be coached. They will turn people down because the person they're coaching won't listen to what they're instructing them to do. The coach is interested in helping you because that's their job and that's what they want to do. Mentors usually help you because they want to pay it forward.

Mindset, Chapter Ten

Mindset is the ability to put yourself in a position where you know you are bringing value to customers, and you know you are courageous enough to speak at the level of your customer. You're courageous enough to understand that you are bringing them value through the products and services you offer and that you have the right mindset to know you're going to be successful no matter what you do.

You may not be successful every minute, but overall, you're going to be successful because you're focusing on what's helping your customer achieve their goals. It's the mindset of being of service and of knowing that you're going to be helping your customer achieve the goals they need to achieve.

It's also the mindset to build trust with your customer, the ability to have them look to you not just as a trusted advisor, but as a crucial partner who's going to help them achieve their goals. The mindset side of selling is ultimately critical.

Prospecting, Chapter Eleven

For many salespeople, prospecting is the most difficult stage of the sales process. Every sales professional faces the challenges of building lists, understanding what to say, deciding when to call, knowing how to interact or when to use email versus voicemail versus calls versus text.

The whole process of prospecting has changed because the customer has become more intelligent about what they need and what their resources are. That means we must change too. Customers have become more intelligent as to what you bring to the marketplace as a vendor. Many companies hire junior sales professionals to make phone calls to set appointments for the senior reps.

How to get referrals is a big part of prospecting and is not something that everybody excels in. Getting somebody on the phone, embracing them, and engaging them in how you can provide them with solutions is the hardest part of sales. We have some amazing ideas for you in this chapter.

Relationships, Chapter Twelve

When the book *The Challenger Sale* came out, relationships got a bad rap. Well, relationships are critical for a couple of different reasons. People do like to buy from people they like and trust. People do like to have long-term relationships. We've had some guests on the *Sales Game Changers Podcast* who have been with their companies for decades. In some cases, they've worked at their respective companies for twenty to thirty years. And, because of the nature of their customer—government or financial services or banking—their customer has been a customer for the same amount of time. In many cases, the relationship has moved beyond merely business to become social as well.

The value of relationships in sales is both interesting and complex. Many of the sales leaders we've interviewed on the *Sales Game Changers Podcast* can point to people they've worked with for twenty to thirty years. Maybe they worked together at a company and then they went separate ways, and then maybe came back as the companies were acquired. The ability to speak to people because you have developed that relationship is critical.

One thing we don't talk a huge amount about is having fun and enjoying your work. Most people enjoy sales when they're successful, and it's afforded them great lives. But it's the relationships that allow them to continue, and the reason these long-term relationships continue to develop is because value is being brought on both sides.

Research and Preparation, Chapter Thirteen

When we ask the sales leaders on the *Sales Game Changers Podcast*, "What should you be doing to be more successful?" preparation always comes up. It could even be simple. One of our guests, Steve Richard, said you must find three things about the prospect in three minutes or less.

John Asher talks about understanding personal things about the customer before you engage. When people ask, "What is the best way for me to be successful?" or "How can I truly become a great sales professional?" we often tell them to understand their customer's challenges and industry more than anyone else.

Asking open-ended questions is great, yet they have to be effective questions, and definitely not ignorant ones. Your customer is busy, especially the higher they are in the organization, so you need to understand what they're going through. It's not hard to do the research anymore. You can search the internet for information on any industry, and you'll come up with dozens of things that are talked about, including news, regulations, and new developments that have happened.

This chapter will help you see ways in which top sales pros research and prepare for their conversations and give you ideas to improve your own methods.

Value, Chapter Fourteen

Neil Rackham, author of *SPIN Selling*, one of the classic sales books of all time, said that sales has always been about value creation. We know that. We know that customers are not going to be spending their dollars if they can't see the value that you're providing.

It's been that way since consultative sales was created but it's even been there more critically over the last couple of years because the customer has access to more information. By searching the internet and social media, and talking to peers and other sales reps, the customer sometimes feels that they do not even need to speak with sales professionals. It's now more exigent that sales professionals bring extreme value to the customer not just for what the customer needs to accomplish today, but for what the customer needs to accomplish with their customer and their customer's customer for the foreseeable future.

This is more critical as we go through this mass shift where many industries are developing and changing. It's critical that you truly think about the value you're bringing—not from your perspective, again, but from the customer's perspective. How is this value bringing them solutions that will help them achieve their goals and grow their business?

We cover a lot in this book. I'm happy that you're here to come along for the ride. Let's get started.

Prologue

This book contains excerpts of direct quotes from more than 500 *Sales Game Changers Podcast* interviews completed from 2017 through 2022. The complete interviews can be found by visiting www.salesgamechangerspodcast.com and searching for the guest by name.

CHAPTER 1:
Leading Customers and Salespeople to Success

Questions to Ponder:
- *Do you have what it takes to be an effective sales leader?*
- *If you are a successful sales rep, do you have what it takes to move into a leadership role?*
- *Are you willing to sacrifice your own financial reward to help others achieve theirs?*

Strong leadership needs a strong foundation. Part of that foundation involves setting the vision and strategy, coaching your team, and overseeing the work while considering how you can raise everyone's game.

Several sales leaders on the *Sales Game Changers Podcast* have offered the following strategies.

Angela Rakis helps companies grow their sales process:

> If you're managing a team, you have three jobs—leadership, setting the vision, and strategy.

> It's managing, making sure the tasks get done. It's coaching. It's getting your team to see more in themselves than they currently see in themselves. [You can help] them see the bigger vision, letting them know you believe in them and helping build their confidence.

> *Episode 358, May 4, 2021*

We've had a lot of leadership experts on the podcast give ideas for sales leaders. **Amy Su**, the author of *The Leader You Want to Be,* was one of them:

> If you're the leader of a sales team, how are you raising everyone else's game? . . . For many folks, they were once the star sales individual contributor. Now you're moving from being player to coach.

Are you taking the time to share all the things you've learned? [Are you sharing] the pattern recognition and all the tools you've gained over time across your sales team?

The goal is to create a team of rock stars like yourself.

Episode 394, August 17, 2021

As you move out of an individual contributor role into a leadership role, you'll have to approach your work differently than before. That includes how you hire for roles and, over time, how you help develop your people.

Many of the sales leaders we've had as guests on the podcast led teams around the globe or in specific industries, such as the public sector.

Nick Bollini has led many successful sales teams:

[When you move into leadership,] you've got to make a conscious decision to move out of being an individual contributor where you're focused on you and your own personal achievement. You move into that space of, how can I take what I know and have a positive impact on a team? . . .

Episode 098, September 24, 2018

Effective communication is another part of a strong leadership foundation. Good, direct communication needs clarity of focus to create effective leadership.

Todd Albright leads a global sales organization that has received many industry-wide accolades:

All [effective] sales leaders have clarity of vision, good communication, good leadership skills—written and oral. But I'd say that two things probably stand out: the ability to identify the objective and to harness the organization focused in that singular direction . . . No matter where you are in the organization, [it's easy] to get distracted by extraneous stuff that's not going to move the needle or deliver the result you've committed, so a clarity of focus [is important].

The reality is, great leadership [is] having a plan [and] executing that plan . . . You start to realize that, whatever you're selling, you're selling to the individual needs of the people in the room.

Episode 245, June 23, 2020

Activity and accountability are necessary. For example, if you haven't completed something, be specific about when you'll do it instead of just saying you'll get it completed one day.

Dan Maier is a seasoned sales leader:

It's about activity. You've got to have a high level of activity if you're going to be successful in sales, and you've got to make sure you manage your time to be able to drive that activity.

The second thing is you've got to be accountable. Sales leaders like myself are always looking for people who want to move up. I look at those that are accountable, and that can be both in a positive sense and in a negative sense.

If you don't get something done, don't say, "I didn't get it done." But say, "I'm going to get it done by this date, and I commit to it." And then you fulfill that commitment.

You've got to take chances. You've got to learn from mistakes.

Part of being in sales is taking risks. If you're not taking risks and you're risk averse, you're going to have a real hard time scaling your career.

You've got to be genuine, because customers do business with salespeople that they trust.

Episode 191, November 11, 2019

Direct communication, not passive-aggressive communication, helps sales professionals gain trust and build a cohesive team.

Bob Dunn is a well-respected public sector sales leader:

There's nothing worse than an individual that's passive-aggressive, because you never know where you stand. People that work for you never know where they stand, and I don't know that you can build a cohesive team with that approach.

The more direct [and] the more honest you are with people, the better it is for them. . . . Whether that's building them up because they're doing a great job or helping those that are struggling to be better. The more direct you can be and the more honest you can be, the better off you will be as a leader.

Episode 107, November 7, 2018

Some of the guests were leading women sales thought leaders, including Alice Kemper, Colleen Stanley, and Amy Franko.

Along with direct communication, observing what happens in a live conversation with your team and prospective customers can help you help your staff improve results.

Alice Kemper:

It's important that leaders observe [conversations] in real time, because when a sales rep comes in your office and says, "Here's what happened on the call, I said this, they said that," you're getting [only] half the story. They don't remember all the questions. You don't see the facial expressions, the body language, all those kinds of things.

Episode 353, April 19, 2021

Emotional intelligence, discussed further in another chapter, plays into the role of a leader. As a mentor told **Colleen Stanley**, "Stability allows ability":

Great influence in selling is a combination of physiology, psychology, and consultative selling skills or leadership skills. It starts with emotion management. As a mentor told me, "Stability allows ability."

When we're able to remain stable, we don't get flustered, we don't take things personally, we don't start making up stories about the prospect [or the person we're coaching]. Then, and only then, can we execute the right coaching [and] selling skills.

Episode 249, July 7, 2020

When you or your team have good calls and improve your skills in that area, you're better able to be the "calm in the storm" and become the strategic and trusted partner for your clients. As a result, clients will find more value in you as a person and partner.

Amy Franko:

Our job as a trusted adviser to our clients and to our prospective clients is to be that calm in the storm . . . Agility and being strategic . . . can help you be that for a client or a prospective client. . . . So much of sales is about communication and thinking about how we're communicating with our prospects, with our clients.

The key takeaway from this part of the conversation is looking at the skills that we need to be building in ourselves and, if you're a sales leader, the skills that you want to be looking for in your current team and as you're hiring into the future.

You do have to know your product, and you have to know your stuff. [Otherwise,] it's going to be hard to have credibility. It's also going to be hard to be agile when questions and problems are thrown at you.

When you know your products well, you'll be able to make quick decisions and marry that with solid communication skills for good results.

As a sales professional, there's a lot more that I see you needing to bring to the table today . . . it can't just be the charisma factor, you have to bring all of it—your expertise, your selling skills, your communication and leadership. And, as a leader, you have to be able to develop those skills and coach those skills in your team.

Episode 283, October 26, 2020

Whereas some organizations may struggle due to how the sales, marketing, and operations teams have different—or even opposing—goals, a company that operates from a main leadership tenet can stay on track and succeed together.

Carrie-Anne Mosley has led teams at some of the top tech firms:

We're all about customer obsession. That's our No. 1 leadership principle and, as a company, we live by leadership principles, which have an amazing result not only on our customers and their businesses, which we add significant value to, but also internally.

It's an interesting phenomenon. The leadership principles aren't just something that we hang on the wall here. It's something that every employee—sales, operations, from the person at the front desk to the person on the top floor—we all live by these leadership principles and we use them in our day to day. What it creates is a very frictionless sales environment, which is nice, because I've been in organizations where you felt like the sales team had one set of goals and various teams within the company were almost working against them. We don't have that here, because we're all working around these common leadership principles.

To have the top leadership principle be customer obsession is also a wonderful situation for me, because over the years I've built great customer relationships.

Episode 189, October 29, 2019

Mark LaFleur was the second interview we ever did:

You want to make sure the entire company is aligned around the mission and vision of the business and, if you have that, then it's all about hiring talented people and inspiring them to do great things.

Episode 002, October 11, 2017

A combination of accountability and autonomy can help members of your sales team thrive.

For example, **Raza Latif**, a leader in the government contracting industry, mentioned that you can lead or motivate someone by allowing them to figure out their path:

Sometimes mentoring is about letting people shine and letting them figure their course out and then you stand behind them.

Episode 036, January 22, 2018

Leadership and empathy work together. Empathy and caring for our team will help us receive the best from our people. Creating an environment in which people can communicate, collaborate, and cooperate is what **Chris Bishop** aims for with his team:

As sales leaders, we need to approach the professionals that we have working for us with a bit of care and concern. Simply beating them over the head is not going to be a recipe for success . . . I'm encouraging them to stay focused [and] keep up the momentum.

Our customers' missions aren't slowing down so neither can we . . . Ask for help when you need it. Communicate, collaborate, cooperate more than ever before. I'm trying to create an environment that allows people to feel that way.

Episode 296, August 19, 2021

When we've done everything we can as a leader to help someone and failure happens, what do we do? In what ways do we create a space in which our team can share their concerns and struggles with us so they can improve without fear of reprimand?

Andrea Waltz is the author of *Go for No*:

> [We need a] cultural shift around the idea of what is failure. And are we okay with hearing "no"? And do we, as a sales team, talk about those no's and do we bring those no's up and say, ". . . I'm having difficulty with rejection. . ."?
>
> But also, culturally, is it something that we talk about?
>
> Is it the elephant in the room, or do we talk about, "I'm getting no from this person. What can I do to move past it?"
>
> [Tactically and psychologically,] what can we do as an organization to get better about handling those but also being willing to talk about those things?
>
> . . . Leadership in general needs to shift the culture.
>
> *Episode 264, August 25, 2020*

Relationships matter. When you care about your team members and empathize with them, you can set yourself up in a position to help them move forward in their careers and increase employee engagement and satisfaction.

Chris Baron, author of *The Fearless Leader*:

> I often like to remind people that "leadership is not a title." [Leadership] is how you show up every day, so my strength has always been around bringing the best out of people and getting them to believe in themselves enough so that they can deliver maximum productivity.
>
> I also make sure that I'm focused on relationships—[so focus on] relationships inside your organization, relationships outside your organization, relationships with your customers, with your prospects, with your peers, with your bosses.
>
> These relationships are so important in order to deliver the things that you're trying to deliver, because none of us can get there on our own. We all need support. We all need guidance. We all need customers, and this is all, in my mind, fundamental to the relationship-building skills.
>
> *Episode 113, December 12, 2018*

As the COVID-19 situation evolved, some leaders found themselves shifting focus to embrace the people side of leadership more than they had before. Even as COVID-19 retreats into the past, the skills and knowledge we gained during that time prove useful.

Chris Krackeler is a sales leader in enterprise software:

> I've always been focused on results, as well as the people that are driving and making the results possible. This year my . . . pendulum is shifting more to the people side as opposed to the results side.
>
> As a leader I've wanted to be authentic . . . and I want to know how the team is doing. But we don't need to pretend that this [first pandemic] year is normal. It's okay for it to be hard, and I wanted to do what we call "connection conversations" with my leaders and the broader team to understand what people are going through, what they're feeling, what's going well, what they're struggling with.
>
> I've done a series of focus groups with marketers and people in customer success and sales on the ground. I want to understand what's working, what's not, what they want to see more of from Blackbaud, how we can help them right here, right now, and how we can be the best possible place to work.

Episode 304, December 17, 2020

Excellent leaders ensure everyone's voice is heard—not just the loudest voices.

Cynthia Barnes is the founder of the National Association of Women Sales Professionals (NAWSP) and a well-known proponent of the women in sales movement:

> I have advice for the women, and I also have advice for leadership.
>
> The advice for leadership is ask yourself, "If the women are not speaking up, have I, as a leader, created a safe environment for them to do so?"
>
> One thing that they did in . . . [a past] presidential administration was, when they had executive leadership meetings, the women would say something and then a man would interrupt them and say the exact same thing, and [people] would say, "That's a good idea."
>
> What they started doing [to counteract that] was having a buddy system. [In the buddy system,] a woman would say something, and then her female counterpart would say, "Jackie, that's a great idea."

And it would affirm and solidify what she said. Unfortunately, that's what it took for women to be heard.

Episode 288, November 9, 2020

Leadership involves learning from diverse views and welcoming diverse thinking and skills, as sales leader Nancy Bohannan mentions.

Nancy Bohannan:

For me, what leadership is all about is leveraging those people around me who are different. . . .

[One team member's] personality is very different than mine, so we have the male-female [difference and others] and he's become one of my go-to guys on my leadership team, because I want his perspective.

I jump to the gun kind of quick, and he's very thoughtful. For me, diversity is all about pulling the best out of everybody to get the best answer . . . Fundamentally, you . . . have to believe that famous quote "Strength lies in differences, not in similarities." If you can internalize that and believe it, it's so easy to embrace diversity.

Episode 330, February 23, 2021

It's also important to be intentional about seeking out diverse people.

Rakhi Voria is an emerging sales leader with success at IBM and Microsoft:

As leaders of sales organizations, it's important for us to be intentional about seeking out . . . [diverse] individuals and thinking about our recruiting processes, even the job descriptions that we're writing . . . and taking out some of the masculine language that might be in there.

I see some job descriptions out there that say they're looking for people who have a competitive sports background and, as I think about myself, I can barely throw a ball much less catch one. I probably would have seen that on a job description and not applied for the job. These little edits make a big difference when we're trying to widen the pool in terms of hiring.

Episode 237, May 28, 2020

> "There's so much noise. Ignore the noise, and get to the basics. Sales is still about the basics. It is still about managing the conversation that you have with a potential client."
>
> —*James Yeager*
> *Episode 158, June 17, 2019*

> "When you think about the things that you can control, it's your mind, your attitude, [and] your opinions. You can't control what other people think, or luck and karma—if you believe in that, good luck. Realistically, things happening in the world . . . we can only control how we react and respond to those things. A lot of it is just mindset and constantly reminding the team of what they need to be focused on right now, in the moment."
>
> —*Jason Rozenblat*
> *Episode 325, February 11, 2021*

After failure, leaders stress that trust and helping team members identify what they learned continue to help sales professionals grow in their careers.

Javier Vazquez and Courtney Bromley have had long and successful careers for Microsoft and IBM, respectively.

Javier Vasquez:

> I give my leaders and give the sales folks the ability to experiment and try new things, but the most important thing coming out of that is, "What did you learn if something didn't go right?" Then pick yourself back up and go right at it. . . . I want to make sure I see passion and tenacity to reach those results.
>
> Whether you're a leader or whether you're an individual contributor, be part of a positive learning culture to help you and your peers to be more successful. That creates the space for new ideas and creativity and I see the rewards. It sounds hokey, but I've seen it in action, and that positive learning culture will pay dividends in the medium and long term.
>
> *Episode 273, September 25, 2020*

When you create trust with your team, they'll feel more comfortable coming to you with challenges and to ask for your input. Ideally, you want to develop a team that feels comfortable seeking you out for advice and counsel.

Courtney Bromley:

> If [you're] a leader . . . who is open, collaborative, and willing to help and get involved while admitting that you don't know everything and you're willing to take constructive criticism, you'll be the kind of leader that people want to come [to ask for help]. . . . They want to get your advice . . . so if you could be that person that is a nice colleague, a good mentor, willing to help when people ask, then you also will probably be the kind of leader that people want to come and work for or be on their team."
>
> *Episode 324, February 9, 2021*

By establishing that trust and listening to your team, you create a positive learning culture that helps everyone change the game for the better.

We touch on empathy throughout the book, because when we know how to empathize, we can listen and build better connections with our staff, employees, and customers.

Jennifer Ives spoke on empathetic leadership and empathetic sales:

> You need to be human with your teams, and you need to feel where your clients are and understand [them] from a human perspective

and from a business perspective . . . You've been working with them. They're your current clients. You know better than anyone what they were experiencing in the past and then where they are today. And, if not, then it's important to be part of those teams . . . [to] lean in, help them understand, and help guide them through that.

. . . Persistently check in with both your teams and . . . with your clients. We're hosting lots of conversations with our clients. We want to be sure that we're offering simple pieces of advice, because many times, when you are in a state of crisis or you're in a state of panic . . . those simple reminders [and] pieces of advice are important.

The simple advice doesn't mean that it's not complex, and that's why they're having challenges thinking through that.

She also advises actively making offerings.

Don't just say, "Is there anything I can do to help?" [Instead say,] "Here are the things that I see you are struggling with. Here's what's going on in the industry. Here are the ideas that I have for you. . ."

. . . To be honest, it's not about growing the business. It's about supporting them and understanding where they are and making sure that you can add value to those conversations.

Again, be proactive, do not wait for the call. Call them. It's empathetic leadership.

Episode 222, April 15, 2020

"The enlightened sales managers and sales leadership understand that they want their salespeople out doing what they're good at, what they're paid for. They take as many of those non-revenue generating activities off their salespeople as possible."

—*Mark J. Silverman*
Episode 371, June 14, 2021

Surround yourself with good people. Hiring and good leadership contributes to ensuring that happens.

Josh Abich has had a lot of success building new teams:

My approach with respect to leadership and developing people is sometimes you have to build and create that talent. . . . We don't have the expectation that everybody's coming in as an A player. But we do need to find people that are aligned with that in principle.

We also need to find people who align well to the culture, to the vision, and to our mission. . . . Finding that is difficult but that's something that we strive to do and continue to do on a daily basis.

Episode 046, February 14, 2018

Meridith Elliot Powell is a well-known sales speaker and the author of *Thrive: Strategies to Turn Uncertainty to Competitive Advantage* and *42 Rules to Turn Prospects into Customers,* among other books:

Jack Welch, the legendary leader of GE, used to say that, as leaders, we need to focus on three things: cash flow, customer experience, and employee engagement.

But I argue that Jack Welch led in a much different time when we had more time and more resources, because if you focus too much on cash flow, you can alienate customers and employees. But, if you focus your time and your energy on employee engagement, you'll drive an incredible customer experience, you'll build an unbelievable team, and you'll [also] drive cash flow.

[Salespeople] are dependent upon the people who work around us.

Learn to lead through the power of the question. You get to decide what you need and what you want, but [you decide] when you ask people how. You simultaneously give them voice and responsibility. You give them skin in the game. You turn on intrinsic motivation.

You want that customer service department to go to the mat for you. Get them involved. Tell them what you need and then ask them how to deliver that. They're going to be a part of your team . . . who you surround yourself [with] is an unbelievable competitive advantage.

Even if they don't directly report to you, you have unbelievable influence over that if you stop telling and you start asking.

Episode 269, September 11, 2020

Shawn Rodriguez leads sales teams pursuing business with state and local governments:

> For any sales leader . . . open sales capacity, open head count makes hitting the mark so hard, yet you must practice discipline and patience in making sure to hire right and avoid the temptation to just hire fast.
>
> Some companies don't afford you the opportunity to be patient to hire right. They want you to hire fast, so finding that middle ground can be extremely difficult.
>
> If you want to be a sales leader . . . be sure to gut check why.
>
> If you aren't willing to give up the glory and truly contribute through others, then you should consider continuing to be the best sales rep you can be. I've worked for executives who felt if you didn't want to be the CEO of the company, you're not motivated enough, and I could not disagree more.
>
> Stay true to yourself and your passion and be authentic. Finally, find ways to give to the culture of your company, not just take from it."

Episode 200, January 13, 2020

Gary Newgaard points out that recruiting and hiring is something to work on every day. He has led organizations at Compaq and Oracle and has built companies:

> The hard part [of leadership] is finding great people and hiring great people and then enabling them to overachieve and help move them through their careers, so staffing is something that you have to do every day.
>
> It's not something you do when you have an open rec. We're continuously networking, making new friends, getting leads on qualified people.
>
> LinkedIn is a great social media way to meet people and stay abreast as to where the shakers and the movers are.
>
> You've got to surround yourself with strong staff.
>
> You don't lead by sitting in your office. You need to be out, about, working with your business partners, working with your sales teams, working with the marketing, the PR teams.
>
> You just have to stay engaged and be willing to be that person that can take out the trash and also stand up and give a speech, but [still] be available [and] be visible all the time."

Episode 052, March 9, 2018

Global sales speaker **Ron Karr** asks, "What would the world look like if everybody acted like a leader. . .?" This self-reflective question can help leaders determine what they need to work on or do:

So who's a leader? You are a leader. Salespeople are leaders. Your managers are leaders. Teachers are leaders. Parents are leaders. Coaches are leaders. In fact, if you want to be brave enough, everybody in this world is a leader, because we should be leading our own lives. . . .

What leaders do is, after something happens or goes on that may be below what they expected, they don't blame others. The first thing they do is they ask this one central question:

"What could I do differently next time?"

Episode 391, August 10, 2021

Sharing specific tactics with your team can inspire them to take actions like the ones **Colleen Stanley** talks about below:

As a sales leader, I'm going to give you a tactical practical. [Let's say] you've got upcoming group sales meetings [and] upcoming one-on-one coaching sessions.

I would craft out your tactical sales management questions . . . "What was the pain? What was the business problem?" And then I would craft out emotional intelligence skills.

- How are you? What's got you worried?
- What do you think is getting in the way of you executing?
- Where's instant gratification showing up where we need to apply delayed gratification?
- What's making you afraid of asking for what you need [or] a next step?

. . . I would take a look at your pre-call planning and say, "Do I have questions planned to get into the mindset of my seller and then do I have questions planned for the skill set?"

Second, I would say, if there is a person or a situation that you're frustrated with right now, ask this question—and actually Charles Eisenstein posed it—"What's it like to be you?"

And, even if you don't agree with it to the best of your ability, write down what it's like to be you. That's the first move towards empathy.

Episode 249, July 7, 2020

CHAPTER 2:
Account Planning: Your Future Self Will Thank You for Being Strategic

"Do today what your future self will thank you for."

—Greg Davison
Episode 370, June 10, 2021

Questions to Ponder:

- *How committed are you to helping your customers achieve their goals?*
- *Are you regularly consulting with other team members on how to help your customers?*
- *How much time do you spend thinking about your customer's business and how you can help it grow?*

Over the years, guests on the *Sales Game Changers Podcast* have shared their wisdom and learnings about providing more value for existing accounts. Naturally, sales reps find it easier to grow an existing account instead of starting from scratch by prospecting for new accounts.

When it comes to value, it's not a one-way street. To *gain* value from any account, we must consistently and proactively *provide* value to the customer. It's not their job to ask for it. We need to proactively research their industry, ask questions, listen, and be aware of their needs and any changes in the marketplace. While "value" may be an overused word, it's an important concept when it comes to the topics of account planning, strategy, and development.

Whether prospecting for new business or growing an existing account, the sales leaders we interviewed for the podcast have agreed on the importance of putting the customer's needs first. To you, this may seem obvious, yet putting it into practice isn't simple, especially if a sales professional is in the early stages of their career. When you need to make your numbers and the pressure is on, it can be easy to forget these lessons about customer-centric planning.

Sales leaders use the term "extreme value" to refer to the level of knowledge, empathy, experience, understanding, and caring that a sales professional needs to bring into a client relationship. Throughout this book, you'll see wisdom and tactics shared on related topics, such as empathy and leadership.

Customers are always learning, so we must do the same. They do their research through the internet and social networking—often before engaging with a sales rep for the first time—so it's necessary to be prepared and ready for their high level of knowledge. With existing customers, it's equally important to be prepared. They expect it, and they're assessing whether you're still the best partner for their company.

As part of this "extreme value," the sales professional of the future needs to understand the challenges of their customer—and of their customer's customer. People don't have loads of extra time these days. If they don't understand the ways in which you can help them, and how you can continue to help them, they'll look around for new solutions that may not include you.

As a salesperson, you're in the profession of solving problems and providing services and products to support your customer's problem-solving efforts. Part of that is understanding your customer's goals and incorporating your knowledge of those goals into your account planning, development, and strategy. By doing that, you're putting the customer first. Part of account planning is gathering information and, if needed, evidence to help them understand how you're still the ideal solution to help them achieve the goals they have.

You don't have to do the account planning alone in a silo. Getting together with colleagues in marketing, your sales team, and even with technology partners can give you a full view of where customers, and their offerings, are headed. This is done in order to bring that extreme value we talked about. On top of that, projecting out a number of years into the future helps you understand how you can partner with your customer for the long haul, and it gives you the info and understanding of how to communicate that to your existing customers.

This book exists, in part, to help sales professionals know what to do consistently in order to prevent those stressful moments of wondering how they'll make their quarterly numbers. Part of that begins with getting ahead of the situation.

> ## "Don't wait for things to happen. Make them happen."
>
> *—Liz Heiman*
> *Episode 452, January 3, 2022*

Sales expert **Liz Heiman** suggests how being proactive can be an effective way to manage communications and relationships. With a proactive approach, clients know you have their interests at heart. She notes that, by getting ahead of things, you may help them figure out what they want, and it may be something bigger than you originally thought:

> Don't wait until tomorrow, don't wait for them to call you, don't wait for [customers] to tell you they have a problem. Don't wait, get ahead of it. . . .
>
> If we're waiting for [customers] to call us and order, we're missing the opportunity to get ahead of solving their problem and helping them figure out what it is they want. Or, they may order something way bigger . . . if we get ahead of it instead of waiting for them to call us and tell us what they need. . . .
>
> If somebody says, "I'm going to call you on Thursday" and they don't call you, don't wait for them to get around to it. They're busy. . . . Get in touch with them. Don't wait for things to happen. This is the core of being proactive: Be intentional, know what you want to do, make your plans, and then don't wait for things to happen, make them happen."
>
> *Episode 452, January 3, 2022*

Being proactive, as Liz Heiman recommends, is part of managing yourself. Patrick Narus advises managing yourself to ensure you're doing all you can to create success for you and your team. When you're doing that properly, you'll be proactive while also holding yourself, your team, and your clients accountable.

> ## "When the customer succeeds, you succeed."
>
> *—Patrick Narus*
> *Episode 393, August 12, 2021*

Patrick Narus was an emerging sales leader when we met him:

> Everything starts initially with managing yourself . . . you need to make sure you're doing everything in your control to ensure success for yourself, your team, and your organization. And of course, naturally, the customer. When the customer succeeds, you succeed.
>
> It's the consistency which is the difficult part, but once you get good at it and you can get a routine down, it works like a well-oiled machine.
>
> *Episode 393, August 12, 2021*

A plan helps you to keep going and to achieve the consistency and routine that Narus said would work like a "well-oiled machine." Below, seasoned sales leader **Joe Markwordt** mentions the importance of having a plan combined with focused activity. Both elements need to exist to achieve success in sales:

> Have a plan. My mantra is, "If you don't have a plan, you will become a part of someone else's plan." This is true in sales, and it's also true in life.
>
> . . . It doesn't matter if [salespeople are] going into a prospecting call [or] if they're going into a closing call, they should always have a plan for that call.
>
> - What are the goals and objectives of the call?
> - What are the questions that you need to ask?
> - What are the outcomes you're looking for?
>
> You should have a plan for your territory, a plan for your account, a plan for the deal, a plan for the meeting.
>
> Just about everybody in this business has a quota. They have an annual goal attainment they're looking for. They want to be able to

manage their revenue. They want to have a quality pipeline. I kind of flip it. I say it all begins with focused activity.

If you want to make your goals, get up every day and have a plan for that day and have a plan for your territory, plan for your accounts, plan for your meetings. The pipeline is a good indicator of how well a salesperson is doing in their territory, but the most important aspect of the job is what we're actually doing each day. . . . If salespeople just master these two things, they will be very successful in their career.

Episode 048, February 21, 2018

You can move plans from the white board into action and become an "essential mission partner" as Akamai's sales leader **Randy Wood** notes below:

For me, personally, there's no better sense of satisfaction and accomplishment than developing a sales strategy for a market or for an opportunity, creating shared vision and real passion . . . for pursuing that strategy and taking that plan off the white board. . . .

You can see lots of plans sitting on a white board and that's where they die. So the ability to take the plan off the white board and put it into action, and to execute, and then to go do great things and have great success—there's nothing more satisfying than that. It's getting an order on the last day of the quarter just before midnight, or [it's when] you know you're making a difference for me, for the leadership of this team, for the company's success, but ultimately for the success of your customer. . . .

You can find strategic plans for large government agencies online. By versing yourself in an organization's mission, you can enter a conversation with a prospect with a tailored approach based on what's most important to them. Account planning helps you put the customer first, which results in more success.

Episode 164, July 15, 2019

Michael Lewis played lacrosse in college and took many of the lessons from the field into the sales process:

Start macro and then build down to the agency's mission to understand what they are in business to do and what is that agency's purpose and mission. Once you've established what that mission is, you can then take a look inside of the agency's strategic plan . . . [The plans are publicly available.]

You will find all kinds of opportunities [related to] the challenges that the agency is faced with and then bring it down to your individual prospect. If you are calling on an executive-level person, they have a certain set of challenges that they're faced with, as opposed [to] if you're calling an operator who is responsible for operating and maintaining the records management program.

I would customize the approach depending on who you're calling on in order to connect with that individual on their level and what's most important to them.

Historically, or from a reaction perspective, I find initially people may go in wanting to tell people about their service and what those benefits are. Invariably, if you're not connecting, you're not moving the opportunity forward, so it's a question of . . . flipping it around to their perspective.

Episode 146, April 30, 2019

Brian McGuinness provided interesting ideas:

I believe that leadership and doing the right thing and motivation is contagious. I believe that outstanding people have one thing in common and that's an absolute sense of mission: "Let's accomplish the mission."

Sales professionals are remembered for what we give back [and] how much we care [by focusing on account development].

Episode 187, October 21, 2019

Account planning is a future-focused activity that focuses on your customer, your customer's customers, and what your company is looking to do.

Government contracting business development expert Nyla Beth Gawel shares an acronym, B-O-L-D, to help people be future-focused:

- Be Future-Focused
- Orient around Outcomes
- Learn about Your Company
- Drive with Data

Nyla Beth Gawel:

The acronym is be bold, B-O-L-D. [The first letter] stands for *Be Future-Focused*. What's coming for your customers and what is your company looking to do? Those two parallel paths: be future-focused and look out for what's on the horizon.

The second is *Orient Around Outcomes* . . . Think of [sales] as that end outcome that you want your final customer and your company to achieve.

The L is *Learn About Your Company*. I spend a lot of time on corporate strategy, and people say, "What's our strategy again?" Engage and ask. If you don't know who your corporate strategy leaders are, if you don't know what your corporate strategy goals and objectives are, ask and learn, and make sure you understand it, because it's important to what you're communicating to your customers.

The D in BOLD is . . . *Driving With Data*, and data comes from everywhere. It doesn't just come from our marketing leads, our inbounds, and our outbounds. Be the sensor, drive yourself with data by paying attention to what's happening in your surroundings and what's happening in your customer's arena, and bring that together. I'm very confident that, if you can follow that and be BOLD, everyone here is going to definitely be able to continue down their successful path.

Episode 395, August 18, 2021

Greg Davison favors doing today what your future self will appreciate, creating a simple, single-page account plan, and sending proposals that align to the customer's problems:

I like to say, "Do today what your future self will thank you for." In other words, do the hard work now.

In the context of sales, what does that mean?

It means get into your account plans. And I'm not a big fan of three-page plans. The plans that we have with my teams are on a single page, because it's more about the dialogue and the interaction of the team than it is the written [plan]. . . .

[It's about] calling the hard customers that you just haven't gotten around to. You do that hard work now so that your future self will say, "Hey, I'm glad I did that last week."

You're a culmination right now of all the decisions that you've made. . . .

Go and put time on your calendar for when you're going to go do that cold call that's scaring you half to death. Put time on your calendar with peers. Maybe order up some Uber lunch . . . and work on account plans for an hour. But do it with some people and have some fun with it.

Episode 370, June 10, 2021

As you work through your planning, you'll find multiple opportunities to pursue with only limited time to pursue them. When you have more opportunities than you have time to handle, sorting through them in order of priority will save you time.

> ## "Prioritize the ideal customer that's got the shortest sales cycle and the most likelihood of buying."
> *—Liz Heiman*
> *Episode 452, January 3, 2022*

Liz Heiman and Alice Heiman both come from sales thought leadership royalty, Their father, Stephen Heiman, was the co-author of the classic *Strategic Selling* and the founder of the sales training company Miller-Heiman.

Liz Heiman:

Prioritize—figure out who your ideal customer is, figure out what are the most important things you need to do.

Take all of those other things that don't matter and put them on the back burner but do the things that matter.

Prioritize the customers that are going to grow. Prioritize the ideal customer that's got the shortest sales cycle and the most likelihood of buying, and prioritize out those customers that are wasting your time and are never going to buy from you.

Episode 452, January 3, 2022

Throughout this chapter are numerous ideas you can implement in your account planning and overall sales techniques. Alice Heiman shares her 5x5x5 "secret sauce" for complex sales.

Alice Heiman:

Quite a few people do have a complex sale. . . . I'll just give you my secret sauce now . . . I do [something I call] "5x5x5."

[In other words,] I start with five companies that fit my ideal customer profile, and all of you probably have that somewhere at your company. . . .

You may have what's ideal for each product line. It could be a manufacturer that has many distributors. That could be your ideal customer for one. And then, in another case, it could be a company that has many locations across the US that are not distributors.

Whatever your ideal customer is, it should be made up of the demographics and the psychographics of who would most likely buy from you and who will be an ideal customer for you once they buy from you.

When I have that [ideal client information], then I make a list . . . of 50, 20, or 100, whatever size list you need to hit your quota. . . . Then, I pick five at a time. This is what some people call account-based approach, account-based selling, [or] account-based marketing. It's an account-based approach.

What I will do with those five companies is find a minimum of five people at each company. Sometimes I find eight or three, but I try to find five or more, because I know with these deals, it's going to be complex. I will then take that company, and I put them on a spreadsheet. . . . Then I go on LinkedIn, search the internet, go on their website [to] find the five people who have the titles that usually buy from me. You all know what titles usually buy from you.

Then, I get a few peripheral ones, too, that may not be the exact person, but might be somehow involved . . . Now, I'm ready to go. That's the five companies, five people from each company.

Now, I'm going to make multiple contacts on multiple channels for a five-week period. I figure, by five weeks, if I've left a couple messages, sent a few emails, done a few LinkedIn requests or interactions . . . if they don't want to talk to me, they won't have responded to any of them.

That's how I do it: multi-touch, multi-channel for five weeks. I start on LinkedIn.

Episode 365, May 18, 2021

Matt McDarby is the author of numerous sales books:

Stick to the process, know the behaviors that are going to work, that are going to get the outcomes you want. Stick to them. That's what I mean by being systematic. And make time to do things like planning your calls effectively and reviewing your results with your coach, getting feedback, getting better every time. . . .

Because I'm an executive, I get messages on LinkedIn constantly, email outreach, phone calls from people that it's a one-way push. "This is what I do. I'm going to help you with lead generation." I get 100 of those a day, and I will respond to many of them. And I'm certain that 99 percent of them are not reading, not listening, not understanding my feedback. If they did, it would be competitively different. They would stand out.

To be elite, be systematic and keep your ears open.

Episode 325, February 11, 2021

CHAPTER 3:
Every Sales Interaction Is a Conversation That Grows a Relationship

"You want people to say, 'Wow, that is the best conversation I have ever had with a salesperson, because they didn't sound like a salesperson. [They] sounded like somebody who had my best interests in mind, who gave me what I needed to know, and showed how they could help me on a regular basis going forward. . .'"

—*Dave Kurlan*
Episode 408, September 20, 2021

Questions to Ponder:

- *How committed are you to helping your customers achieve their goals?*
- *Are you regularly consulting with other team members on how to help your customers?*
- *How much time do you spend thinking about your customer's business and how you can help it grow?*

Success in sales involves having the right conversations with the right people at the right time. That includes engaging in conversation with the right partners, influencers, or team on the customer side.

To consider:

- Are you prepared?
- Have you thought through what you want to be saying to them?

- Have you thought through what might be of interest to them?
- Do you have notes?
- Have you worked with your team to understand what you need to do when you're out there engaging in these conversations?

Outstanding sales professionals know, in a conversation, that they're providing value to the customer, and they need to communicate that to them. Even customers you've been working with for years, if not decades, are challenged with more problems than they've ever been challenged with before. Conversations can help both of you unpack problems that you can solve with your company's solutions.

More to think about:

- Have you learned enough about your customer so that you understand the acronyms they might be using?
- Do you understand some of the code words or jargon they use?
- Have you reduced your own jargon or expressions that don't add value?
- Do you practice your conversations?

On the *Sales Game Changers Podcast*, we talk deeply about how to communicate the value that you're bringing to an existing or new customer and to note:

- What they need to hear
- What questions you need to ask
- When the customer needs to hear about a particular topic

Through conversations with customers, you have opportunities to distinguish yourself in a way that helps both buyer and seller determine good ways to move forward. Read on for suggestions around how to have powerful and effective conversations, starting with what to say.

Shelley Row is a successful sales and leadership speaker:

Two of my favorite phrases are, "Say more about that" or "Tell me more."

Then, it does draw in more of that conversation and then you can do that reflective listening to verify that the content being exchanged is correct.

One of the most powerful ways that I used reflective listening is when I was coaching a staff member, or perhaps we were having a performance problem. We would have a conversation about performance . . . and I would say to the staff person, "Now you say back to me what you believe we just agreed to do." . . . It gives you the opportunity to clarify.

Pay attention to when you're sensing that context, that emotional piece in your communication, and try validating that emotion that you observe by speaking it out loud and checking to see if you understood that emotional context.

See if it then lowers the brain activation, so you can have a more constructive conversation.

Episode 318, January 25, 2021

Brian Harman has a very large social media following:

We want to relate with people on a human level over the challenges we've overcome. If you want to have those conversations with your colleagues, or even with your potential clients or current clients, you can ask them, "What's the biggest challenge you've overcome in your life?" That's one way to build relational trust.

Episode 297, December 1, 2020

Although you should do research before your conversation, you only need to have it "about right" and not 100 percent perfect, according to John Asher. Through doing that research, you can start and engage in a productive conversation.

John Asher is the author of *Close Deals Faster* and *The Neuroscience of Selling*. He was a frequent guest on the podcast:

If you do great research with a buyer before you interact with them, after rapport building, you can start with, "Here's my understanding of your needs." Bullet, bullet, bullet. Whatever they are. Ask a simple question like, "Do I have this about right?"

The research at Harvard shows you don't have to have it perfectly nailed. You just have to have it about right. If you do, in 95 percent of the cases, it causes a big conversation between the buyer and the seller, which naturally morphs or gravitates into the needs analysis and, as opposed to being very frustrated, the buyer is very impressed.

Episode 404, September 9, 2021

When we have these conversations, we're aiming to forge a relationship and connection. We want to sound human, as Dave Kurlan says.

Dave Kurlan is the author of *Baseline Selling* and is an industry leader in sales hiring assessment. On the podcast, he talked about urgency:

> You want people to say, "Wow that is the best conversation I have ever had with a salesperson, because they didn't sound like a salesperson. [They] sounded like somebody who had my best interests in mind, who gave me what I needed to know, and showed how they could help me on a regular basis going forward if we partner."

> How do we be the person, the company, the team, the organization that this prospect, their colleagues, that company says . . . "We talked to these people before, and they were just like everybody else, but this time, what a breath of fresh air!" Or, "We brought in a group of salespeople, and we brought in a salesperson that we had never met with before. Wow, that was the most unique conversation we ever had with a salesperson."

> *Episode 408, September 20, 2021*

You can use storytelling in conversation to clarify what the customer needs and describe the outcome in a way they can visualize and understand.

Bill Donellan is a top sales leader in the public sector market:

> You can use words like these to ensure you have the story straight:

> "Are we here to have the same conversation? Let me tell you three quick stories about three other Adobe customers that faced the exact same challenge, and I'm going to explain to you how they solved the problem. Then we can talk about how you're similar or different from each of those and see if there's a path forward for us."

> In that context, I know that this organization is trying to do A, B, and C, though I say, "The FDA did it this way, CDC did it this way, the Census Bureau did it this way, and this is how they described the problem they were trying to solve. This is how we solved it and this is the outcome that they had as a result of that. Does it sound like we're talking about the same thing?"

From there, you can have a real conversation about their real problems.

- What do you have to do to set this project up so that it's going to be successful?
- Who from your team needs to be involved?
- Who from my team is going to show up?
- How long is it going to take? What kind of interaction do we need to make sure it stays on track?

Those are all the kinds of conversations that we're trying to have as early as possible to make sure that expectations are right and we deliver value and meet the customer's expectations.

Episode 310, January 7, 2021

If you know why people should want to talk to you, instead of the other way around, you put your prospective customer first. That can evoke more empathy and compassion for them on your part and lead to a more productive conversation overall.

Jason Rozenblat:

Be compassionate. These are people on the phone. They're dealing with a lot of things just the same way we are. So instead of looking at them as a prospect or customer, or just another means to hitting your number . . . try to be compassionate and genuinely care about the customers and what's going on with them.

Create that line of communication where you can get that feedback directly from the field or from wherever you're able to get it, but then go out and seek the truth so that when you are making a suggestion to a leadership team, to a board, and then convincing the rest of the group that you're doing it, there's data to support those decisions.

Episode 325, February 11, 2021

Lee Salz is a successful author on books urging sales professionals to differentiate themselves, including *Sell Different* and *Sales Differentiation:*

If you apply that same approach to sales, what I call sales crime theory, we don't pick up the phone, we don't send a prospecting email unless we can answer this question:

Why should they want to have a conversation with us right now?

. . . That means we need to do some research so that we can personalize the outreach and reach that 82 percent who've said that they've taken a meeting with a salesperson who had contacted them through some type of prospecting means. That's just one example of the overall strategy development that salespeople should have.

I get calls all the time from executives, sales managers, CEOs, business owners saying, "We've got a closing problem," and what they don't recognize is that closing is rarely the problem. It's a symptom of the real problem, which is poor discovery.

If you don't have effective discovery conversations, then you don't have the tools, as you move through the process, to keep the energy in your deal.

Once we know what the outcomes are that we look for, then we can put together [the following]:

- Questions we're going to ask
- Information we're going to share
- Obstacles we may encounter in that
- A plan to address them

We need to have strategy development . . . we should always have strategy in place before we're picking up the phone or [before] we're going to meet with folks.

Episode 233, May 11, 2020

You may know what words to say in your sales conversations, yet what do we want people to feel before, during, or after the conversation to help us build trust and understanding? Comprehension can get us to that point.

Listening, paying attention, and demonstrating active engagement can build trust with customers and colleagues alike.

At times, sales professionals may think or worry about the quota to the detriment of the conversation. The worry can negatively affect listening and other parts of the conversation in a way that erodes trust.

Sales leaders including Brian Egenrieder and Monica McEwen were invited onto the podcast numerous times.

Brian Egenrieder:

You had to understand what people were coming in for that hard drive for. Ask them questions about their use. Is it gaming? Is it work?

. . . You can sell them things that they need—not just because I'm getting a bonus because they're walking out with seven or eight different items in their hands. It's helping them do [it all in] one trip, and they like you more for it. That taught me a lot.

What I learned early on is to create a conversation and make sure there's comprehension in that conversation, so it's not just saying words. It's making sure they understand what you're trying to convey. Make sure you understand what they're trying to convey, which builds trust and builds a dialogue that ultimately helps you learn about what they need [and] what you can do for them and, [as a result] you're selling them on value.

Episode 179, September 23, 2019

Monica McEwen:

This might be a little bit controversial . . . Don't make your quota the only thing you think about, especially when you begin a conversation with a prospect. Instead, think about how you can be of service to the people that you meet.

Too many salespeople are quick to rush the sale in conversation before understanding if they're even talking to the right prospect. So take time to ask lots of qualifying questions to understand if this is a prospect that you can serve. . . .

Think about your understanding of the customer's problem . . . if you have something that can help with their problem and have intimate knowledge of that customer, and you can bring them compelling value, you're going to get to your quota. So think more about how you can serve the individuals that you're speaking with as opposed to how to close the sale.

Episode 054, March 12, 2018

Mark Hunter is one of the top sales speakers of the past few decades. His books, *High-Profit Prospecting* and *A Mind for Sales* have been consumed by tens of thousands of sales professionals around the globe:

It's about having the conversation.

There are two things you have to do with any conversation . . . you have to have a conversation that creates trust and a conversation that creates empathy.

What does that mean? That means listening.

I want you to listen to the other person's opinion and value it more than ever . . . There's nothing new about this, but nobody ever did it because we were too busy selling.

Now, it's about listening.

What you want to do is . . . create that relationship, because . . . here's what happens . . . I create authenticity by being empathetic and trustworthy, because then people are going to see me as being authentic.

They don't want to deal with a fake. A fake doesn't create trust.

When I'm seen as authentic, then they're going to open up, they're going to share more with me.

Episode 226, March 23, 2020

Speak less, yet still take a leadership role in the conversation. Customers and prospective customers appreciate an efficient and well-run conversation. They also look forward to getting insights on how to make their business more successful from sales professionals, so focus on that.

Jane Gentry:

I am much smarter when I speak less. Let me say that a different way: customers think I'm smarter when I speak less. It's a lesson that salespeople need to learn.

We don't always have to do the talking. In fact, we should not be carrying the conversation the majority of the time, and it's a problem I still see in young salespeople.

Episode 132, March 11, 2019

Kim Harrington:

I see the biggest deficit is in the area of taking control of the conversation, and I don't mean in the sense that you're in charge . . . but [that] you're the expert.

If you are the expert at something, rather than just fielding questions that may lead nowhere, it's important for you to take a leadership role in the conversation. To me, the very best way to do that is to just gain permission to ask questions.

Episode 086, July 19, 2018

Focusing on deep conversations and authentic relationships is the way to go, and you can still have a personality. In fact, it helps you create relationships.

Mark J. Silverman is the author of *Only 10s:*

Having shallow conversations with more people is not going to get you further. You're not doing yourself any favors by touching as many people as possible as shallow[ly] as possible.

Rather than getting into [shallow] relationships, asking the questions you need to ask of what's going to make them successful [will help]. What do they need in order for the sale to go through? What are their goals and objectives?

Episode 371, June 14, 2021

Judy Schramm helps companies build out their LinkedIn presence:

If you want to build real authentic relationships, then what you want to do is allow some of your personality to come through—some of the things that are unique about you.

For example, we have some clients who are in a rock band outside of work. We have another one who restores and races antique cars. We have one who was a ballerina and plenty who've done crew, or soccer, or football. Actually, we had a pro baseball player also. When you can see these things on their [LinkedIn] profile, that is a great way to spark a conversation and build some rapport at the beginning of a conversation.

Episode 405, September 13, 2021

Gigi Schumm has led sales teams at major technology organizations:

It is about understanding the needs of the business or organization or person you're selling to, and how what you have to offer—whether that be a product or whether that be a service's offering—can help meet those needs or alleviate the problem that the customer is dealing with.

Being able to engage in those conversations, recognize those needs, and have that bridging or translating conversation . . . is the essence of what being a good salesperson is.

The other components of emotional intelligence—like persistence and resilience, the ability to bounce back and the ability to take some criticism—are hugely important when it comes to having a long career in sales.

Episode 008, October 8, 2018

Even if you have stellar conversations with prospects, they may not choose your services or products. When you have numerous relationships and a full pipeline, this won't be a catastrophe. In fact, if you're keeping up with your pipeline, you can move on to the next opportunity and continue building relationships there.

Jeffrey Wolinsky is a successful media sales leader:

Finding clients, having conversations, and coming to the conclusion that some of those people won't buy from you is okay. You just need to have more relationships and always be finding new ones because the consistent theme . . . is that things change. And so, establish relationships with people who might give you [a] "no" [while knowing that it] might only be a no for now. [Create] that relationship that starts where you understand their business . . . and become valuable to them . . . [Although it might] result in no for now, [it could] becomes "yes" at a later point in time.

Episode 011, November 1, 2017

CHAPTER 4:
Urgency: You Need Compelling Reasons to Act

Questions to Ponder:

- *Are you committed to helping customers solve their problems without being asked?*
- *Do you procrastinate more than you'd like?*
- *Are you passionate about what you're selling?*

Without urgency as part of the sales process, you'll struggle with getting the customer to move forward. Sales organizations need to sell, and they need to bring in revenue so that the company can continue to perform. You'll need to help customers understand the urgency and the cost of not moving forward, especially during times when companies may be delaying purchases.

What will you do to demonstrate and define the urgency in a way they understand? To reiterate, we need to help our customers solve *their* customer's problems and help our customers in solving their customer's *customer's* problems. If you can show them how your solution will help them move their business forward, you're going to be in a much better situation.

Dave Kurlan, author of *Baseline Selling*:

It's magical when the prospect and the salesperson both have urgency. There's alignment, and the sense is that they are collaborating together to get something done.

When only the salesperson has urgency and the prospect doesn't, the salesperson will be seen as pushy and tone deaf.

When only the prospect has urgency and the salesperson didn't uncover it, the salesperson will be seen as unresponsive and not listening.

So it's crucial that we have both urgencies in place and marry them up and work together.

Urgency comes from the impact and the monetization of their compelling reason to buy. When you uncover that, that is like unlocking the buried treasure.

Episode 408, September 20, 2021

In your sales conversations, find a way to articulate the cost of not taking action in a way that doesn't come off as overly pushy. Bake that information into all parts of your sales presentation, because it will come off as pushy if you only mention it at the end.

Mike Schmidtmann is a top sales trainer and mastermind leader:

Urgency needs to be built in at the beginning of a sales presentation—beginning, middle, and end . . . If you throw urgency [in] at the end, you're being sales-y and pushy, so I pull. . . . [I'll define what I meant by that.] You push by telling. You pull by asking. I pull. So, in the beginning—and I call this a triple close—you use the quid pro quo.

"If you like what you see and the price is fair, can you take action in thirty days?"

You do this again in the beginning, middle, and end. You cannot do it at the end if you haven't done it in the beginning, because otherwise you're being pushy.

Again, urgency must be built in at the beginning, middle, and end.

Ask them what needs to happen. You ask it innocently. You give them a reason for taking action and why it makes sense to do it now. Nothing works 100 percent of the time but that'll probably double your close rate.

Episode 202, November 16, 2020

Gil Cargill is a veteran sales professional:

Be prepared with an elevator speech. Let's shorten the sales cycle to create a sense of urgency on the part of you and your customer.

You have to always understand and be able to articulate the cost of a "no" or "not now" from the customer's point of view.

What does it cost your customer to say "no" or "not now?"

Episode 363, May 17, 2021

You want to target those who feel urgency and those who find your work valuable. This will save you countless hours.

Caryn Kopp is an expert on sales prospecting:

> You want to target a group of people who not only feels urgency, but who also will find you to be the obvious solution. Once they know that you exist, they wouldn't even take a step without you being part of their decision set.

> They just need to know about you and will also willingly pay what you want to charge for your services.

> It's very few people who hit my doorstep that sell on price. Most of the people who hit my doorstep want to sell on value. But not everybody out there is going to pay for value.

> What if you could very efficiently stop talking to people who would never willingly pay what you want to charge for your services? Think of how much more efficient you'd be.

Episode 332, March 1, 2021

Without urgency, stagnation can happen.

We can use "thoughtful urgency" on ourselves in our own work, so that we can serve our customers well.

Matthew Cannone is an emerging sales leader:

> The most important and underrated element of being in sales is being thoughtful. Try to balance operating with a sense of urgency, but take a step back. Maybe do not respond to every email on your phone, and sit down at your computer and think about it. Gain a more credible opinion before you voice your flavor of it.

> . . . Stay curious, operate with urgency, follow through on what you promise the customer. Be thoughtful. Lead with empathy and do it with a smile on your face, and good things will come.

Episode 393, August 12, 2021

CHAPTER 5:
Creativity: Yes, Anyone Can Be Creative . . . with Practice

"Creativity starts with listening."

—*Jose Palomino*

Episode 267, September 4, 2020

Questions to Ponder:

- *Are you an idea person?*
- *Do you like to brainstorm with team members and partners to come up with innovative ideas for your customers?*
- *Do you look for new ways to get things done, to out-think your competitors?*

We started hosting four Sales Games Changers virtual learning sessions per week as the COVID-19 pandemic began. In addition to our *Women in Sales, Sales Leader,* and *Optimal Sales Mindset* shows, we started the *Creativity in Sales* webcast, about how you need to be creative in sales. We started the show because sales changed when the pandemic started. What had been done in the past wasn't going to work at all or in the same way as before. You'll notice our guests touch on that subject throughout the book.

As sales professionals during a challenging time, we needed to figure out strategies and ways to continue to show value to customers, so we created the webcast to talk about how to be creative regarding every aspect of sales.

Your customer will hear a lot of the same pitches, especially if you're in a competitive situation where the customer has asked for numerous vendors to present solutions. Most proposals and pitches will sound alike, which can lead a buyer to focus on price. Since that's a race to the bottom, we're sharing what expert sales professionals suggest you do instead.

Instead of sounding like all the others, how can you show up differently? It's worth thinking about how to come up with meaningful ways to show the customer what you can do for them. We believe that creativity is a huge asset of elite sales professionals—especially as the time we have in front of the customer decreases.

To consider:

- Are you developing new ways to help your customer understand the value that you're bringing? In your presentations, are you creating new ways to show that you're thinking differently and out of the box?

- Are you showing new ways to provide value quickly and easily, so your customer understands how you're helping them?

- What creative approaches could you take when it comes to outreach?

- In what ways could you use creative methods to forge relationships?

As odd as it may sound, you can even find ideas from childhood and use them to develop highly creative outreach.

Karen Galvin shared the following on one of our shows:

1. Bring people back to their childhood.

Go to the toy store, walk up and down the aisles, see what you can see, and see if it relates to your product or service. Or see if it relates to a conversation. . . . Sending a hula hoop with a note that says, "I'll jump through hoops for you" [is one example].

2. Ideas are everywhere.

[In an Atlanta hotel,] they put this tiny little bottle of Tabasco [next to my eggs] and, of course, I go into my creative mode, thinking, "Are my products and services hot stuff? Can I send this in an envelope to my prospects and clients and tell them that I'm looking to make them hot stuff with their clients?"

I grabbed it, and I've been ordering them ever since. They're tiny little bottles, and people get it in the mail and they think, "This is great." I sent an oversized tennis ball to a client that was doing an event at Citi Open, and it said, "Let me be supportive of your efforts."

Greatbigstuff.com sells huge pens and huge everything that you can imagine. . . . You can send a huge pen. Just think big.

Somebody sent me jumbo playing cards, and I'm thinking, "COVID. People are playing cards. They're doing puzzles. What could I say about this? What could be so creative?"

Inside, there are of course the cards and the jokers, so I can send this and say, "We're not joking around with regard to providing great service."

Episode 397, August 24, 2021

If you're ever worried about not knowing how to be creative, it's something anyone can learn to do. It takes practice, and you'll become better at it as you use the creative part of your brain more often.

Alan Stein Jr. helps high-performing business leaders grow based on his years of helping high-performing basketball players take their level up a notch:

When I'm on stage, there are times that I try certain things, and it doesn't work as well as I'd like. So then I go back and I workshop it and I try it again . . . in a slightly different way. . . .

If it's still not working, then maybe I shelve it, or maybe I continue to tweak it until it does work.

Episode 248, July 1, 2020

Your creativity, according to sales leader **Chris Cutino**, will give you the chance to be successful in your career. You can use creative approaches for any aspect of the sales process:

It's your creativity that's going to give you the ability to be successful within your role. So if you point a good rep in the right direction, give them the tools, but also let them be creative. As long as they're using the right morals and certainly staying within specific guard rails, it's amazing what you can learn from the people around you.

I'm amazed every single day by the creativity of salespeople that have been on the job for a year and they come and they say, "I tried this, and it's amazing the response that I'm getting, and I roll it out to the entire team."

Episode 056, March 16, 2018

Creative endeavors sometimes have been born out of desperation or hard times. If times feel difficult, consider what creative step you can take to stand out in a positive way. Combine creativity with listening for effective results.

Gigi Schumm:

> [As an example, one account] issued an RFP for their biggest requirement. It was a database [and they chose the competition].
>
> That's where I got one of my favorite sayings, which is "desperation sometimes creates creativity." [Instead of packing my bags and giving up, I listened to the customer.] I got to know them at all different levels and understood from a big picture what they were trying to achieve.
>
> [The CIO of the agency] used a slide to illustrate visually the architecture that he was trying to put into place, and I realized, as I looked at that slide, that there was an opportunity for us to become part of what I will call their "plumbing," their standard build across the agency.
>
> *Episode 043, February 6, 2018*

You can find some of your most creative ideas while doing mundane and everyday tasks.

Ryan Brown:

> What's actually happening is your brain creates neural highways when it's doing something that it recognizes. . . . If you've ever heard anybody say to you, "I have my best ideas in the shower," it's because their brain has gotten off on this neural highway. . . . All these resources have suddenly freed up for the creative parts of your brain to start working.
>
> *Episode 070, May 3, 2018*

Try brainstorming when you feel stuck, and try working in short bursts to be more productive.

Tom Snyder is a world-renowned sales expert and the author of *Escaping the Price-Driven Sale:*

> The brain does not do a good job of bouncing back and forth between creative ideas and judgment. If you're going to brainstorm,

you need to set a time . . . [three to five minutes] and just let your brain stay on the creative side . . . [without judgment].

Write down any idea just as it comes to you. Then, when the bell goes off, look back and strike out the 80 percent that were ridiculous or impractical. That way, at the end of the week, you'll have a couple of good ideas . . . The effective folks are working in [short and focused] bursts as opposed to scheduling a whole day or as opposed to scheduling even three or four hours at a time.

Episode 266, August 31, 2020

Incorporate creativity into your work. If an effort or attempt doesn't work, you can always change it and try something else.

Trevor Vale:

Creativity has to be incorporated into everything we're doing right now.

We have to be creative in how we address new circumstances. We have to be nimble, and we have to be able to pivot. All good ideas are great until they're not, and we have to be prepared to change what we're doing. So, as a salesperson, . . . if what you're doing is not working, try something else."

Episode 253, July 17, 2020

CHAPTER 6:
Succeeding in Sales with Emotional Intelligence

Questions to Ponder:

- *Do you believe that empathy and emotion management are the keys to building strong relationships with your customers?*
- *Would a sales culture that embraces feedback and change through the development of critical emotional intelligence skills help you grow?*
- *How can emotional intelligence build resilient sales teams?*

The IES was one of the first organizations to invite Colleen Stanley, author of *Emotional Intelligence for Sales Leadership: The Secret to Building High-Performance Sales Teams* and *Emotional Intelligence for Sales Success,* to the stage. During her engagement with us, she helped the sales professionals in attendance understand the importance of what some derisively call "soft skills," such as empathy and accountability.

The development of soft skills rooted in emotional intelligence improve sales leadership effectiveness. Throughout this book, numerous sales leaders talk about the importance of being empathetic and understanding of customers. The COVID-19 pandemic increased our awareness of what people are experiencing in their personal lives, and that may have led to an increased awareness and understanding of empathy. Now, maybe more than before, it's critical to hire for and develop emotional intelligence skills in sellers and leaders.

You can develop and use your emotional intelligence to understand people's needs better. That allows you to "build a story of how you're going to help," as Sam McKenna shares below. This ties into how to construct the conversations you have, because the story you create will become part of the way you illustrate how you can help your customer.

Sam McKenna helps companies build out their sales processes:

If you understand people, you understand the dynamics of their company, their teams, their challenges, what they're measured by, and how what you're selling is going to impact them. You can start to build a story of how you're going to help them . . . and get them to their goals.

Episode 028, December 21, 2017

McKenna recommends advancing your customer in some way while not feeling afraid to have those conversations with them. You can ask them how they're measured annually and then share how you can help them reach those goals. To gain a deeper understanding of them, you can ask questions such as:

- Do you know people within my network?

- Have you worked in and purchased from us before?

Understanding the dynamics of the answers and how to connect the dots is important.

By being aware of yourself and tuning into what others are saying and thinking, you can connect with your customers. The knowledge you glean from your emotional intelligence can inform your understanding of why someone may or may not be moving forward with you.

Colleen Stanley:

[Emotional intelligence] starts with that awareness of what . . . you're feeling, what the emotions are from those thoughts and . . . it's being equally tuned into what others are thinking or feeling, how that might be affecting their emotions, and how they show up taking action or inaction.

Episode 249, July 7, 2020

Alex Bartholomaus is the author of *Endurance Executive: A CEO's Perspective on the Marathon of Elite Business Performance*:

My focus is elite business performances, and that is the nexus of taking someone's performance around emotional intelligence . . . and then connecting that with process . . . a lot of times people are quick to point out the process side of the equation, and that is important. But what's also important is investing the time and energy in yourself, nurturing yourself . . . [being] vulnerable, and working on your emotional intelligence—in particular, self-awareness and self-regulation.

. . . Whether you're in your twenties or you're in the zenith of your career, you can't spend enough time in this area, and we oftentimes find that, thanks to our expertise, we can always make a difference in this area, because people just don't spend enough time focusing on it.

Episode 041, February 2, 2018

> ## "Happiness is a daily activity."
> *—Paul Smith*
> *Episode 185, October 15, 2019*

To increase and improve your emotional intelligence, Paul Smith suggests finding a sense of presence with regard to knowing who you are and what you like to do.

Paul Smith, former GM of Red Hat's Public Sector Division, was the recipient of the Lifetime Achievement Award from the IES in 2017:

> What we find over time, in terms of EQ (emotional intelligence), is trying to get a sense of presence in terms of knowing who you are [and] what you like to do. Because happiness is a daily activity.
>
> Some of the neurotransmitters [like serotonin] that fire off when you actually feel like you're needed [by helping people or engaging in philanthropic endeavors] . . . that's the happiness people need to pay attention to. And these are things that are well documented in a lot of research, and it's real science. That's how I try to ground myself.
>
> *Episode 185, October 15, 2019*

Gigi Schumm points out that, in an ideal mental state, we can weather the ups and downs and the inherent unfairness of the sales process:

> Sales is inherently unfair.
>
> There's always going to be somebody who has a better territory, a lower quota, gets lucky, a blue bird flies in their window—and sometimes you're on the winning end of that. Sometimes you're on

the losing end of that. And so, if you can't make peace with the inherent unfairness, it can make you crazy. . . .

[Sales] is full of ups and downs. It's full of wins and it's full of losses. You're going to have good quarters and bad quarters, good years and bad years. And, again, it's a mental thing more than anything else. If that is going to make you crazy, then this is not the career for you. You have to be smart to be in sales. You have to be empathetic. You have to be a good listener.

[You need to have the personality traits or mental states mentioned above.]

Episode 043, February 6, 2018

The ideal mental state for sales also requires the ability to manage emotions no matter what comes your way in life.

Denise Hayman sees emotional intelligence "as the ability to manage emotions no matter what life has thrown at you":

It means that you have to be aware of those around you. You can't just be dealing with your own emotions. You've got to be dealing with not only what's going on for you, but what's going on for them.

In sales, we deal with this all the time. We have issues that come up. We have last-minute purchasing situations, contract situations. . . .

Do you go into tell mode? "I'm going to tell you how you need to change this." Or do you go into "Hang on, let's back up here and have a real conversation about what it is we're all trying to accomplish and where we are" to tie them back in?

That ability to step back with some maturity and use your emotional gifts . . . to be able to change that situation around . . . are all things that are breakthrough situations around that engagement.

Episode 277, October 11, 2020

Triggers in yourself are something to watch out for, so you can know what they are and how to manage any emotions around them.

Colleen Stanley:

When you study negotiation [and] the people that are experts on this . . . they will include emotion management. It allows you to execute the tactical skills of negotiation, so the emotion management is not allowing a trigger [to affect the situation].

If you want a constant in life, people are going to trigger you. Places are going to trigger you. . . . What we can change is . . . [whether] we decide to react [negatively] or respond with grace. That's when emotional intelligence and emotional management comes into play.

Being aware that the reptilian brain can overrun that logical brain in a nanosecond [means] we've got to be aware to manage that reptilian survival response.

For sales leaders today, you have to . . . [ask], "What is the fear that is driving this behavior?" Maslow's hierarchy of needs [is worth considering here. In that model,] the first need is safety. [Safety and] security must be met. [When those basic needs aren't met, it's that] reptilian brain that causes some inappropriate behaviors.

Episode 249, July 7, 2020

Triggers and having our buttons pushed go hand in hand. GV Freeman points out how situations and people that push our buttons let us know where we need to work on ourselves.

GV Freeman helps sales professionals ground themselves with mindfulness development skills:

One of my mentors frequently reminds me: It's not their fault for pressing my buttons, it's my fault for having buttons to press. . . .

One of my teachers . . . says the world is a curriculum for the soul. [In other words,] every person, place, thing that I interact with has an opportunity to press my buttons. And without people in my life, without employees coming to me and demanding help, without my VP of sales saying, "You haven't hit quota," . . . I wouldn't know where my work is.

Episode 384, July 25, 2021

High emotional intelligence allows you to put yourself in someone else's shoes (important for empathy and listening), and it allows you to build consensus (especially important for leadership and conversations).

Karen Cantwell:

It's important to have a high emotional intelligence, because you're constantly doing consensus building and putting yourself in the other party's shoes.

[Try asking: What are their drivers? Since it's a third party, you may not have the intimate knowledge of the workings of what their metrics are.]

It's a good thing to ask, "What are your metrics to achieve success working with my company?" It's important to be able to discern and relate and be open-minded to other perspectives.

Episode 311, January 10, 2021

500 inspiring interviews with amazing people in the books!

A show at WTOP's glass-enclosed nerve center. I showed up with my microphones and recorder. We decided to use their equipment.

EPISODE 419: Gina Stracuzzi Shares the Three Key Mindsets of High-Performing Women in Sales Leaders

Celebrating *Women in Sales* with Gina Stracuzzi. A quarter of our shows featured women sales leaders.

Gary Milwit said, "Make everyone you speak to feel important." I repeated that on many shows.

I traveled to Detroit for shows.

My favorite photo with a guest was at Catholic University.

The last in-person interview we did before the pandemic was in DC at the arena.

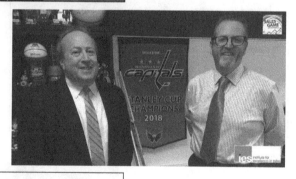

We devoted some episodes to the convergence of tick-borne illnesses, such as Lyme disease, and sales success.

CHAPTER 7:
Understanding What Empathy Is and What It's Not

Questions to Ponder:

- *Do you really care about what your customer is going through?*
- *Can you make the shift to being focused on your customer's needs instead of your needs?*
- *Do you know the difference between empathy and sympathy?*

Often, people think that empathy is the same as sympathy. Sympathy refers to feelings of pity for a person for a misfortune of some kind. Empathy refers to understanding and sharing the feelings of someone else.

When it comes to sales, empathy is the ability to understand where your customers are emotionally and mentally, so you can communicate with them based on that information. During the pandemic, empathy became a hot topic, because transactions decreased and sales professionals had to use empathy to figure out a way to talk to customers and relate to them.

Howard Brown is the founder and CEO of Revenue.io:

Empathy: It's not only critical to understand what it is, it's critical to understand what it's not.

Sympathy has its place, but it's different than empathy.

Empathy is the ability to understand somebody else's emotions—their feelings and their situation—and it's critical. It's critical in my relationship with my wife, with my children, with my coworkers, and with my customers. And it is critical because we all want to be heard.

We all want to be understood, and we want to be seen. It's critical to human nature. It's critical to trust. It's critical to relationships.

When I think about empathy, I think about helping people. And helping people is so critical to the sales process, because at the end of the day, our job as salespeople is to help people make a buying decision. . . .

Episode 344, March 29, 2021

Anyone can struggle with empathy. On the *Sales Game Changers Podcast*, somebody asked one of our guests, "What should I be doing? Because I'm suffering from empathy fatigue." The podcast guest, a VP of sales, replied, "If you, as a sales professional, are suffering from empathy fatigue, take a break. . . . Because that is the essence of successful sales and relationships—the ability to understand where your customer is or the person that you're talking to. Not from your perspective, but from their perspective."

In one podcast episode, **Steve Richard**, a frequent guest on the podcast, shared further ideas on what to do if you're having an "empathy crisis":

If you're having an empathy crisis, in addition to taking a day off, read a [sales] book. . . . Go recharge. Go back to the sales mothership. . . .

Recharge your battery. It's like you're an electric car. Then go back out at it. And then, honestly, if you can't be empathetic and you've lost that authenticity, [and] you just don't care about these people—and I mean this with all due respect—maybe get out of sales. Maybe do something else for a while and then you can come back to it later on.

Episode 234, May 14, 2020

Microsoft's Christine Zmuda added that taking a call while walking—when not presenting to a group—and letting others know you're doing it gives everyone else permission to take care of themselves. Taking time away and taking breaks from screens is important. These moments of healthy movement and "screen rest" allow you to hone your skills at empathy and to have the energy and mental ability to listen deeply to those around you.

Christine Zmuda:

I've tried to be in tune with how people are feeling and how they're managing and also tried to lead by example. . . . [Constantly running from] meeting to meeting without a lot of breaks . . . can be taxing.

You can do little things like lead by example and show people [a better way]. "I'm walking on a conference call where I'm not presenting, so I'm going to have my camera off during this time. I just want to let you know I'm walking." So it gives everyone else permission to get some fresh air. . . If you keep that physical/mental connection, you're going to be better at work.

It's okay not to be okay every day, because we're all going through a lot. If you need a break, I encourage people all the time, take vacation even if you're not going anywhere. Just get off the screens. Take a break.

Episode 346, April 2, 2021

As we continue to work virtually, the challenge increases, because we only see a customer inside a small rectangle on our computer screen. Whether you're skilled at empathy or want to develop it further, it's a critical ability for sales professionals to understand and use. That's why we've included an entire section on this topic for you.

Alice Heiman:

Right now, the best thing we could all do is be kind.

Customers being empathetic to salespeople would be a nice thing, but that doesn't mean they need to spend time with you if you haven't given them a valid business reason to spend time with you. If you cannot tell me in two sentences why it would be worth my time to spend time with you, then empathy [or] no empathy, I don't have time for that.

That's just something you have to become good at—stating clearly and quickly why I should stay on the phone with you or why I should schedule a meeting with you. No, they're not going to be very empathetic to you because they've got all their own problems that they're trying to deal with, so I wouldn't expect them to be. . . .

[Approach] them kindly, because that will give kindness back. So no matter what, if they grouch at you, you're like, "I'm so sorry you're having a bad day . . . Is there anything I could do? Should I send you a funny joke? Anything at all I could do to lighten your spirits?" Be kind and maybe customers will respond a little bit differently.

Episode 295, November 23, 2020

When it comes to empathy, some sales leaders think about how they're helping people. Others point out that empathy is required in cases when you know you have a qualified person on the phone, yet they're saying "no" to your offer. You'll need empathy in the sales conversation to find the answers you need in order to see how to help.

Andrea Waltz:

> If . . . you do have someone who's highly qualified for what you have, but they're still saying no, where does that empathy come in?

> You have to just be human, and you have to try to figure out and ask some questions to learn about their situation and if they are struggling. . . . Sometimes you have to be an advocate. Sometimes you have to help people off the fence. . . .

> If you can help someone in that moment make a decision that might be ultimately best for them, whether you make the sale or not, that's the greatest, most empathetic thing you can do.

> *Episode 264, August 25, 2020*

Empathy is more than merely validating what someone says by saying, "I understand your frustration/situation." You need to understand the emotion and also understand why the person feels that way.

Colleen Stanley:

> [Empathy] is the most powerful influence skill you can learn, and it will be one of the more difficult skills. It doesn't mean that you do not possess it . . . [but we don't often use it].

> Let me give a couple of practical tips. Often, when empathy is being taught, it is being taught to validate a person's position. My philosophy is that validation is skill. It's an active listening skill, but it's not empathy because real-world empathy is where you get rid of the "vanilla" language.

> Let's say I know that you're frustrated . . . I have gone to my empathy class, and I say, "I understand your frustration" and then I think, "Check, I did it."

> [However, to demonstrate empathy is] . . . not only stating the emotion, but it's tuning into why the person is feeling the emotion. First and foremost, we've got to get past the vanilla . . . because the

research is pretty clear. Empathy is decreasing because, first and foremost, empathy is a paying-attention skill.

With all of us being so addicted to technology . . . we're teaching ourselves to be distracted. We're teaching ourselves to pay partial attention.

I might be in a conversation with you, but if I am not fully paying attention . . . I miss the conversation that's not happening. . . . I actually don't have to agree with your perspective, which is the other reason empathy is so darn hard. I might think you're crazy. Doesn't matter. I've got to understand your perspective and demonstrate that I understand it."

Episode 249, July 7, 2020

As Javier Vasquez points out, we don't want to use empathy as a weapon, which means to use it just to get what we want. Jennifer Fisher mentions that she's present with her clients to help solve problems instead of just trying to sell them something.

Javier Vasquez:

We don't want to use empathy as a weapon. It's a valuable sales tool in a sense that it helps you get to the core of what your customer challenges are and offer a solution back, but we can't weaponize it— meaning that you use empathy to just get what you want.

Real empathy is a two-way street of extending emotions to each other.

As a sales leader, if you'd asked me two or three years ago if empathy—listening and feeling—were important, I'd be more focused on what are their business priorities and challenges. But [now I see empathy] is an incredible skill to get traction with your customers and help them accomplish their mission and their goals.

Episode 273, September 25, 2020

Jennifer Fisher:

I want to listen and learn what your problems are and how I can help . . . I look at it as, "Why wouldn't you talk to me? Why wouldn't you want to have me help you with your problems?" I fully believe that, and then in building that relationship with my customer, I'm able to help them.

Episode 126, February 13, 2019

To follow up on what Fisher said, hospitality sales leader **John Washko** says that you can guide customers and be a resource for them. Empathy helps you do that:

> When you're dealing with empathy, the way that you're positioning yourself to move forward is differentiating how you're talking to the customer versus other people in the industry. . . . Guiding them there and saying, "Let me help you walk through these resources, so you can manage up to your organization and let your decision makers see what that pathway forward looks like."

It's being a resource.

Episode 271, September 18, 2020

If you're wondering if you could be more empathetic or want to develop your empathy, the ideas below can help.

Javier Vasquez:

> For the first time in a long time, I have exercised the muscle around consistent empathy . . . [By that, I mean] being empathetic and practicing empathy all the time.

> Just to give you a little personal insight, years ago I took a 360 [assessment], "What are the different attributes of a leader and the personality traits?"

> I scored very poorly on empathy and [at the time] I was a little surprised at that, because I felt like I was a jovial person. I seemed to interact with people well.

> I read through that, came home, went to my most trusted confidant, my wife, and I said, "Honey, I got this survey, and I scored very poorly on empathy."

> What she told me—which is kind of funny—is, "Of course you have no empathy, you're the 'but anyway' guy."

> "What do you mean I'm the 'but anyway' guy?"

> "Well, . . . your best friend could tell you that his dog's passed away, and you're like, 'Oh, that's sad. But anyway, are we going to watch the game this weekend?'"

As I've been working on empathy and the skills, part of being empathetic is exposing vulnerability for yourself and listening without judgment—just listening.

Episode 273, September 25, 2020

Empathy and authenticity work together and can incorporate not hiding that you're a person with a life.

Nyla Beth Gawel:

Empathy goes hand in hand with authenticity for me. Everybody I work with hears me talking about my interns. I mentioned I'm a mom of two . . . It's amazing that they're not banging through this door at the moment. I've learned to have empathy for other people's lives, but I do that through authenticity.

I have to be who I am. I can't hide them.

I can't hide that they've been in virtual school or that my dog's barking at the mail delivery person. I can be authentic myself and have empathy towards others when they are trying to balance and juggle. That's a whole new degree of my own leadership style I've had to put into practice.

Episode 395, August 18, 2021

A lot of empathy is required to work with customers, and interacting with customers—ones who might say no—builds confidence and grit.

Rakhi Voria:

Selling a product or service helped me understand how much empathy is needed for a customer, and the confidence that I built—the grit, the perseverance—every time [I'm] told no.

What better way to develop some of those skills than by having to build a relationship with a stranger? Not only did I develop some of those soft skills, I also was able to cultivate some tangible and hard skills, like how to position, how to influence, how to negotiate effectively.

Episode 237, May 28, 2020

Empathy can focus on your team with regards to celebrating their success and finding out what motivates people.

Bill Rowan is a leader in public sector sales:

You need to figure out a way to celebrate . . . your accomplishments in this new world . . . In an office, we would pull everybody together and . . . recognize someone.

We still try to do a little bit of that online, but I've encouraged people [to do it while working from home]: "Listen, you had a great week, you got a big order in. Share a bottle of wine with your loved one or significant other. Go make yourself a big dinner, turn stuff off, turn the computer off, put the phone down, make yourself a nice dinner at home and use it as a way to celebrate the successes that you're having along the way."

Episode 265, August 28, 2020

CHAPTER 8:
Listening and Questioning: Practical and Powerful Tips and Strategies

"Great conversations come from great questions."

—David Nour
Episode 213, March 10, 2020

Questions to Ponder:

- *Do you often find yourself not really listening, but just waiting to talk?*
- *Are you naturally curious about other people's challenges?*
- *Do you have your questions lined up and ready to go when you are in front of a prospect?*

On the podcast, we would ask, "Why are you so great? What is it about you that makes you a unique and special sales leader?" People often answered with some version of "listening." To capture more about this topic, we began to ask podcast guests, "What is it about you that makes you a great listener?" We've gathered the advice, strategies, and tips shared from our guests here for you to use when you need inspiration or feel stuck.

As we interviewed our sales leader guests, we noticed certain themes show up. They mentioned that we must listen from the customer's perspective. In other words: If you listen deeply to the customer, you can't lose; but you can't listen from the perspective of wanting to talk. You must place yourself in the customer's position, so that you can understand how to bring them value.

> "When there's two people on call, the person who's not talking is the one whose job is to listen. Listen and then ask the customer or prospect to clarify what they meant. That can take the conversation in any number of directions."
>
> —*Kevin Carr*
> *Episode 340, March 18, 2021*

The elite sales leaders we've interviewed have an ability to truly make the conversation about the customer. When talking with customers, expect that you're going to let the customer communicate, and the customer wants to do the talking. Customers will always find more value in what they say versus what they hear from you. To understand how to listen better and ask better questions, let's look at some of the ideas shared at our events.

Gretchen Gordon is a published e-book author and sales blogger:

> You were given two ears and one mouth for a reason, so we need to use our ears a little bit more.
>
> Instead of educating—which is code word for telling—we need to ask.
>
> I don't have any data on this with regards to men versus women, but I feel like sometimes women have to project that they are smart and that they know as much as their male counterparts do, so they feel that turns into telling more . . . if they could just use their talents to ask better questions, they'll have greater success, and they'll honestly look smarter.
>
> If you ask thought-provoking, more robust questions of prospects or customers, you will be placed in a higher position as an advisor. You don't have to come in and be the one that tells people what to do. It's better to ask from an informed position.
>
> *Episode 302, December 13, 2020*

Asking certain questions, and certain challenging questions, can help you be viewed as a trusted advisor.

Denise Hayman:

[A key foundation of being a good sales leader is] to not only ask an easy, close-ended question, but a hard, challenging question. Because our prospects and our customers sometimes need us to do that. . . . We've seen lots of things that they don't see.

Episode 219, April 7, 2020

Doug Brown is the author of *Win-Win Selling*:

The way to get perceived as an expert . . . is asking quality questions that make the eyebrows go up. Make people go, "I want to know a little bit more about that . . ."

. . . Remember active communication. If they're not engaged and we're just giving them the answer, the eyebrows may not go up.

Episode 364, May 17, 2021

As David Nour said, "Great conversations come from great questions." In addition to recognizing we have two ears and one mouth, we can take steps to become less distracted and more centered to support proactive listening.

David Nour is a strategic business relationship expert:

Most of us don't listen to hear. We listen to craft what we're going to say as soon as you stop talking.

I'd say go back to the fundamentals of genuinely getting less busy, less distracted, and more centered—more in tune with being in the moment. So [engage in] much more proactive listening.

Great conversations come from great questions. So if you ask an incredible question that engages, that influences, that shapes the way they think [and the] outcomes they're after, and [if] you invest the time in the relationship to understand the results which they seek and you become an enabler of that, by definition you're going to set yourself apart.

Episode 213, March 10, 2020

Listening extends past our experiences with customers to expand to our teams and colleagues. The critical information we glean from conversations with our colleagues can help us consistently understand what our customers want and alert us to changes in the market.

Jim Van Stone is a sports marketing leader:

> [What's important is] listening to our team, especially the sales executives that we have there on the front lines talking to customers every single day.
>
> We've got to be able to hear [our team] give us feedback in terms of what clients want, what clients are looking for, what challenges people may be facing, what the opportunities are. And sharing that amongst the group . . . is critical and important for us.
>
> *Episode 230, May 5, 2020*

Visionary sales leader **Rob Beattie** shares a tactical way to ensure you keep listening throughout the conversation:

> [To listen better,] take notes. That's a big one for me.
>
> Get a pen in your hand. Have a piece of paper in front of you. Don't do it on your computer, because you'll be banging away, and you'll distract yourself with noise and sound. . . . There's nothing more powerful than being able to go back to somebody and say, "I wrote this down. I wanted to circle back to this." And it's a great way to not forget something and show somebody that you're physically listening to them.

Powerful conversations like the one below can happen due to listening and asking the right questions. Beattie shares a time he went off script to ask a customer to tell him more about something and the positive results afterward.

> When [a client] was struggling [with] recruiting, he wasn't getting enough new people. . . . I just started asking questions, and what it came down to was, he wasn't feeling like he was technology enabled. . . .
>
> The technology at that time would have made a big difference, but I said, "You guys [have] got to figure out a way to become more high tech." And the guy says, "Yeah, I'm just not sure how to do that."
>
> I said, "Well, I got a solution for you. You could put twenty people into this class and maybe they become better at using Microsoft, Excel, and PowerPoint . . ." And the guy goes, "Hey, that's a great idea."
>
> I remember that first moment I said, "Okay, you know what? This is actually something I can do." It was also a huge lesson [that the] script or framework is important, but don't be afraid to move off [script]."
>
> *Episode 203, January 27, 2020*

While going off script makes sense in some cases, you can still benefit from pre-planning the questions you want to ask someone.

Alex Bartholomaus:

A lot of times . . . more junior salespeople ask questions to satiate their curiosity as opposed to asking a question that adds value.

We're getting less and less time with prospects. That applies to just about everybody.

By scripting your questions, you can be precise in asking the questions that serve you the best.

Episode 041, February 2, 2018

Sports reporter and sales professional **Alex Chappel:**

Your questions do matter, because it's going to show your preparation and what you know. . . . It's just being able to phrase a question knowing I have this second question prepared, but if the person I'm interviewing takes me on a different on-ramp where they're going to bring up something else, or maybe they mention a teammate and something they did, be prepared that it's not going to go exactly . . . [as planned].

Also, they enjoy it if you make the interview a conversation [with back and forth instead of having it seem like an interview].

Episode 323, February 8, 2021

Taking notes, paired with asking insightful questions, is the "footwork of sales," as **Alan Stein Jr.** says:

The ability to actively listen and ask insightful questions is the footwork of sales. Because when you ask the right questions, you don't have to convince a client or a customer to buy from you.

If you ask the right questions, and [the prospects] are the right fit, they'll convince themselves to buy from you.

If you can sharpen your sword, . . . your intuition and emotional intelligence, and your ability to ask the right questions at the right time to the right people [to] process the information—and then, based on what they say, offer them another insightful question—you'll just simply drop the breadcrumbs until you lead to the only logical answer, which is for them to do business with you."

Episode 248, July 1, 2020

Active listening moves a step beyond simply listening to get to the heart of the matter.

Jeff Shen helps companies grow business with federal government agencies:

> I feel like I'm a very good listener, but the area in which I feel like I'm improving . . . is that I need to be a better active listener.
>
> People tend to have a thought process of, "If I ask this question, I'm going to get ready to ask another question or I'm going to say something else." People and companies need to be better active listeners to truly get to the heart of what is driving this customer's decision or thought process or how they might buy. Then be thoughtful in terms of whatever they say. Follow it up with something that makes sense.

Episode 125, February 12, 2019

A tactical approach is to use the idea of "five-minute selling" to ask a few questions of your customers on a somewhat regular basis. The approach can help you be seen as a trusted advisor, because you're being helpful and proactive.

Alex Goldfayn is a best-selling author of numerous books for sales professionals, including *The Revenue Growth Habit*:

> For example, throughout the day, you can ask "did you know" questions. . . . "Did you know I can also help you with X, Y, or Z?"
>
> A reverse "did you know" question is, "What else do you need that I can help you with?"
>
> These are three-second questions and, in five minutes during the day, I can ask a hundred of those questions.
>
> We know statistically that 20 percent of them close. We know this because my clients have asked millions of them over the last twelve or so years, and we track it. That means, ask five "did you know" questions—that's fifteen seconds of your time—and you'll close one new line item that will be added over time.

Ask 500 "did you know" questions, [and] you'll add a hundred new line items, and so on.

In five minutes, alternatively, I can call and leave ten voicemails, because my voicemail script takes twenty seconds or so to say . . . [With] the next customer or prospect that you talk to, ask them the reverse "did you know" question. . . .

- What else are you working on that I can help you with?
- What other projects do you have coming up?
- What else do you need quoted?

You might even ask them, "What's on your wish list?" And they're going to give you a list of things. What nobody will say is, "No, I don't want you to make my life easier today."

Nobody will say that. They will all say, "They want to help me."

Episode 300, December 7, 2020

Alice Kemper:

Talking too much is [problem] No. 1. . . . Not asking the best questions is another problem.

Elevating your questions [and not asking] the ordinary questions that every other sales rep out there in your industry is asking [will set you apart from the crowd].

One commonly asked question Kemper notes from advertising sales is when reps ask who the prospect's customers are. Every rep asks that question. So how do you elevate it? Kemper has suggestions. Instead, she says, you can ask:

"What are the three key characteristics of your ideal customer?" That's a thought-provoking question. They're not used to getting it. They have to think, and you're going to get some detailed information.

Episode 353, April 19, 2021

Asking questions can feel uncomfortable sometimes, and that's normal. It's okay to feel awkward and to point out to a customer that you have an awkward question to ask. By labeling it, you acknowledge any discomfort on either side of the conversation and make the experience less awkward overall.

Andy Miller is an expert on hiring sales professionals:

> Forget about being smooth. Just give yourself permission to be awkward and, if it feels awkward, just tell them, "I've got a question I want to ask you, but I have to admit it's going to be kind of awkward." When you label it, they're okay with it, so label it. . . .
>
> Don't wait for the perfect moment. No such thing exists.
>
> What's the best that can happen and what's the worst that could happen? . . . The worst case is never as bad [as we think it will be].
>
> *Episode 309, January 4, 2021*

When you pay attention to others, they're more likely to want to pay attention to you. This follows the law of reciprocity in which people often give back to us what we first give to them. If we pay attention to them, they pay attention to us, and so on.

Charles Green is an expert on trust-based selling:

> If I pay attention to you, guess what happens in your mind? You think, "That was good. You tell me about you." Isn't that the natural thing?
>
> Think about how you go out on a blind date with somebody for the first time, as a weird little metaphor here, and the person says, "Tell me about yourself."
>
> You're supposed to [talk about yourself] because they asked you. It'd be rude not to, but here's the key question: How long do you take telling them about yourself? [The] right answer would be three to five minutes, and that's probably it. Pretty soon in there, you need to say, "But enough about me. Let's talk about you."
>
> We all understand how to do this, but you start by paying attention to the other person. . . .
>
> People don't care what you know until they know that you care. . . . First people have to know that you care and then they naturally become much more willing to listen to what you have to say. That's what I'm talking about by listening.
>
> Pay attention to people for their purposes . . . it makes them much more inclined to work with you. It's how you create trust.
>
> *Episode 270, September 14, 2020*

Listen and learn, and don't feel shy when it comes to asking a lot of questions.

Chris Krackeler:

Listen and learn.

On the listening side, one technique I've used is wait till someone finishes the last word that they've said. Envision that last letter before you interject. We all go into sales because we like to talk.

Always practice listening. It helps you be a trusted adviser and be open minded about learning. You can learn anywhere, from books, from people, from people above you in the org, from peers, from people on your team.

Episode 304, December 17, 2020

To add to that, don't stop asking questions just because it might feel like a lot of questions. **Dave Kurlan** explains more below:

It might take fifteen questions. It might take fifty questions, but you can't stop asking until you reach the destination. You can't be sitting there thinking, "Geez, I've asked ten questions, I better stop." Don't stop.

Episode 408, September 20, 2021

Gary Milwit shares ideas about listening and beyond, which helps your sales process and involves connecting and reconnecting with people with a mind of service before you need something from them:

[Elite sales professionals should be] listening, taking their time, prospecting better, staying ahead of the curve, going back to customers that they've already had earlier in the process to start talking about how they're doing, and then start to build that book before they need something.

Episode 337, March 12, 2021

When you listen, your customers will usually answer the questions you haven't even asked yet. That gives you important information you need to do your job. To help you do this, think about trying to learn something new every day.

Ivy Savoy-Smith is an expert on media and radio sales:

> You've got to be a great listener . . . When you listen, the client—nine times out of ten—will answer the questions that you haven't even asked yet. Being a great listener is something I've learned that, when you're able to do that . . . [it] goes a long way with the client.
>
> *Episode 142, April 15, 2019*

Listen to your market. Below, see some practical tips for ways to listen to what's happening in your industry. This will inform your conversations and the questions you need to ask.

Janet Schijns is an in-demand expert on communications sales and marketing:

> Listen to your market and your prospects. Set up Google Alerts, so that you see what's happening in your industry.
>
> Use the keywords that are important to what you're selling or important to the industry you're selling to. Set up Google Alerts for the companies that you're trying to prospect to, and you'll get a very efficient, effective note every day in your mail showing you exactly what people are talking about. . . .
>
> Engage with thoughtful and insightful commentary, and don't be afraid to just share an article, [such as] third-party expert content.
>
> *Episode 360, May 10, 2021*

Being attuned to the lives and interests of your clients can help you create deeper connections. Karen Galvin took creative approaches with her clients and shares how she did it.

Karen Galvin:

> One of my clients is a CEO, and she said, "I didn't know that I would be doing some homeschooling," and we talked about the fact that she's not a morning person, but she needs to get going in the morning. I saw a mug on cafepress.com . . . and it said, "Homeschool begins after coffee."
>
> I thought that was cute. It wasn't one of those offensive mugs that you can see at times. You've got to be careful [with your choice]. I sent it to her, and she loved it. . . .

Just listen and connect with them.

One of my clients sent a picture of his son in [a] Halloween costume as a lion and I thought that was just the greatest thing. When I had to send him some information, I sent the little boy a card with Simba on it. You can go to Hallmark . . . [or] you can download free clip art from the internet, put it in an envelope, and make your own. Personalize it, listen, and hone in on what they're saying.

Episode 397, August 24, 2021

Instead of calling or emailing people to say you're "just checking in," be more specific, as **Liz Heiman** explains:

Every time I pick up the phone or send an email to a customer, I stop and look at what my last conversation was, and I remind them, "Last time we spoke, you were concerned about this. How is that going? Have you got that resolved?"

. . . They know that I'm not just checking in with some arbitrary thing to talk about. I remember what was going on with them and why it was important. . . . It's really important . . . to be intentional about listening. . . . You cannot be a good listener if you don't care. . . . If you really don't care about your clients, you're in the wrong industry.

It's much easier to listen when you get out of your own head and care about that other person.

Episode 452, January 3, 2022

Sales prospecting expert **Marc Gonyea** points out that one of the key elements of the profession is to treat it as a craft, the way an athlete or comedian does:

If you're a sales professional, you need to review and listen to how you interact with the prospect. How do you sound? What does your tone sound like? Are you comfortable with silence? Do you ask questions? Do you talk too much? Are you not talking enough?

I would advocate listening to your sales calls, breaking them down, including hand-written commentary . . . then asking someone else to break down those calls for you.

Episode 211, February 24, 2020

> "Our best salespeople are those
> that get repeat business from customers
> and those that get references and
> referrals from customers to other
> customers. But it starts with . . .
> establishing trust and being likeable. . . .
> That starts with listening."
>
> —*Mike Maiorana*
> *Episode 100, October 2, 2018*

We've talked a lot about questions to ask customers and prospective customers. What about the questions to ask of yourself? Gay Hendricks shares a "wonder" question you can ask yourself to discover your zone of genius. I've frequently said that his *The Big Leap* is my favorite sales book of all time.

Gay Hendricks:

Grown-up life is a lot about asking yourself the question, "What is my true genius and how can I best express it in the world?"

I'll tell you, if you're in sales, you're in the perfect type of work to do what I'm talking about. I would say that a good half of the fan letters we get for *The Big Leap* are from people who are in sales in one way or the other that have lifted the upper limit off what they're doing and then can function at a whole different level.

You go in that room for ten minutes, and you simply engage in one thing we call a wonder question. . . . We ask [people] to go in and do nothing but say the following question: "Hm, what do I most love to do?"

Actually, we ask them to say the question with the "Hm" and then take two to three easy, slow breaths and then say it again. . . . It sounds kind of silly and weird, but go in a room by yourself and just for ten minutes, focus on nothing but your genius. What is my genius? Just keep living in that question.

Episode 379, June 29, 2021

CHAPTER 9:
Getting Mentored and Coached Are Essential for Career Success

Questions to Ponder:

- *Do you know the difference between being mentored and being coached?*
- *Are you prepared to implement what your mentor will recommend?*
- *Do you have the energy to be coached?*

We've talked with expert coaches about how sales professionals should become more coachable. Before we share their thoughts, I want to give you my take on the difference between mentoring and coaching. When it comes to coaching, you're usually going to receive coaching on a specific topic—phone calls, developing empathy, listening, etc.—that's going to make you more professional and skilled.

> ## "My No. 1 piece of advice for anyone in sales is be coachable."
>
> —*Deana Poole*
> *Episode 403, September 8, 2021*

Coaching requires more of a time commitment than being mentored. With a mentor, you might meet infrequently or when you have a question. With coaching, you're usually meeting on a regular basis—anywhere from once a month to weekly. Either way, for it to work, you have to want to be coached or mentored. That applies especially to coaching. In fact, we work with a lot of coaches at the Institute for Excellence in Sales, and a lot of them say they'll turn people down if they don't believe the person wants to be coached. When someone doesn't want the help, they likely won't listen to what they're being instructed to do to experience success.

When it comes to mentoring, you usually ask someone to take part in that role, and there's no monetary exchange. Maybe the mentor is older than you, and you're asking for their advice. Although you may ask for help in specific areas, you're generally asking for career advice. For example, you might want to know how to advance into leadership or become a more established leader in a certain marketplace. In these cases, you're usually asking someone who's had the expertise in building out that skill or path in your career.

The coach is interested in helping you, because that's their job and that's what they want to do. Mentors usually help you because they want to pay it forward.

We encourage people to be both mentored and coached at some point. Whether you're mentored or coached, you need to follow through on the advice or counsel you're given for any of it to help you.

Before you meet with a coach or mentor, identify what you need. Do you need to learn a new skill? Do you need to develop a new habit? The answer will determine which type of person can best help you.

Tibor Shanto is a sales prospecting expert:

> A coach is absolutely necessary, and a coach doesn't necessarily . . . [have] to be someone external to your company, and it doesn't have to be another sales guru.
>
> I would argue if your goal is to figure out how to change a habit . . . it's about the habit, not about sales. You might be better off for this particular challenge getting a coach . . . who's more focused on individual change management.
>
> *Episode 341, March 22, 2021*

Staying open to learning is something elite salespeople do.

Alan Stein Jr.:

> [What] makes the elite the elite is, as confident as they are . . . they stay very open to coaching. They stay very open to learning, no matter how successful they are. . . .

They focus on those core fundamentals and habits, and they don't deviate from them. Then, lastly, they don't allow themselves to get distracted.

It's not just about doing the right thing. It's also about avoiding doing the wrong thing.

They keep their circles tight. They stay well insulated. They focus on the basics. They respect the fundamentals. They make sure that they're always in preparation mode.

Episode 248, July 1, 2020

Before you seek a mentor, work on building your personal brand. **Nancy Bohannan** is a top sales executive with leadership success at the top tech companies:

You have to build a [personal] brand before somebody is willing to sponsor you and then you have to be clear [as to] what you want.

A great saying that relates to this is, "The best way to get promoted is doing the current job you're in damn well."

Episode 330, February 23, 2021

We've had top sales leaders from technology, marketing services, and professional services contribute to the podcast. Here are some things they say you can do when it comes to mentorship and your growth.

Andrea Cohen is a telecommunications sales professional:

[First,] get a good mentor. . . . Model the behaviors you want, and you'll learn a lot more quickly. . . .

The second thing is, inspect what you expect. That's a lesson you need all the way through. You need to understand that you are doing what you need to do from a funnel perspective, from any perspective, from a deal perspective, and you need to make sure that what you're seeing is actually what you wanted to have happen.

The third thing is to know that customer well. You have to balance the corporation with the customer, but if you lean on any side, lean on the side of the customer. Your knowledge of them will make you more successful.

Episode 160, June 24, 2019

Find mentors who push you to be better.

Patti Dumas is a marketing services sales leader:

> I would challenge any new rep in the field to find those mentors--
> not just people that are above you, but your peers that are going to
> push you to be better.
>
> It's not just people above you that do that. It's what you find in
> yourself and how others do it, and they are now my best friends. We
> travel and do vacations together, and it's just a lot of fun to know
> how we started.
>
> *Episode 181, September 30, 2019*

Christian Woodward has led start-up and established sales teams:

> Find a mentor . . . career development, I believe, is not something
> that you should go totally rogue on and do by yourself. So take the
> time to ask people to contribute to your own success. . . .
>
> Play the long game . . . you're going to be faced with decisions about
> your job, about your career, about customers, about a particular
> deal, and you're going to have to prioritize the short-term game
> versus long-term success. If you want to stay in enterprise sales
> throughout your career, I would keep focused on the long game
> versus the short-term game.
>
> *Episode 067, April 24, 2018*

The long-term game, and thriving in it, involves getting a mentor.

Tech sales leader **Dave Kushner** says:

> Having a sales mentor is key, not only from a tactical business
> perspective, being able to go, "I got this deal that I'm working on
> and I'm kind of stuck," but also from a long-term career perspective.
>
> When you associate yourself with someone who's enjoyed a long,
> successful career in sales, you try to learn as much as you can from
> that person. What I did through the years was, I found myself
> merging things that I learned from my mentors with things that
> I've learned from my own career.
>
> *Episode 140, April 8, 2019*

When it comes to managing salespeople, you must be both a coach and cheerleader.

Andrea Waltz:

> You can cheer so much, but eventually, people have to take action. Our advice is always to focus on behaviors—getting people into action, focusing on the specific things that they can do.
>
> What's so key is to constantly be cheering people and rewarding people for that action, regardless of the result, because so much benefit will be gained from taking the actions. Learning will happen. Progress will happen and, as long as people continue to engage in the behaviors and they're tweaking as they go, eventually those things will turn into actual tangible sales results.
>
> *Episode 264, August 25, 2020*

When you hit the doldrums, finding someone you respect and can emulate can help you figure out the best path forward.

Craig Mueller is a sales mentor to many:

> Sometimes, you hit the doldrums. I would say practice your craft, find somebody—find a coach, find a mentor, find someone that you emulate—and understand how they're being successful . . . Then, by practicing your craft, writing down goals and objectives that you have, and finding a mentor that you can speak to when times are tough . . . [it will help ensure] that salespeople establish and then stay on the right path."
>
> *Episode 209, February 17, 2020*

Dan Maier:

> If you don't have a mentor, go find one. And make sure when you find one that you're willing to listen to some of their feedback versus just checking in or getting a sense of what he or she may think about one thing.
>
> 1. You have to hold yourself accountable to setting up time to speak with your mentor. The opportunity to be a mentee and to get some advice from a mentor isn't when you need it and within the next day. Set up a recurring schedule. Make it something that's habitual. Make it a recurring appointment on your calendar.

2. Bring some different ideas to market. Bring some different sales ideas, some different sales strategies. Then . . . do a little roleplay. . . . It can be hard, but it can be easy to have this successful role-play exercise when you employ the tenets of committing your-self to doing it. It makes you that much better in front of your customers, but you've got to make time for it.

Episode 191, November 11, 2019

Deana Poole is a media and marketing services sales professional:

My No.1 piece of advice for anyone in sales is be coachable.

One of the reasons I've had the success that I've had is I try to not be the smartest person in the room. I'm constantly reading a book, listening to a podcast, watching a webinar, asking questions that no one wants to ask, raising my hand, trying to figure things out.

We just rolled out this cool digital tool with one of our partners in Michigan. I said, I don't understand this. I got on a Zoom with him, and he walked me through it again. I'm a senior salesperson. I am supposed to know . . . but accepting the fact that I don't and seeking people to teach me and remaining coachable every day . . . has given me a little bit of an edge and kept me moving forward.

In any industry, just be coachable and continue to teach yourself.

Episode 403, September 8, 2021

In addition to being coachable, be proactive about being coached. By that, we mean take responsibility to make time with your coach happen. They may be busy, and that should not deter you from asking for their time.

Colleen Stanley:

Be proactive about being coached.

I've seen this scenario play out. We all know the sales leader is supposed to be setting aside time for one-on-one coaching sessions and group coaching. Then, life hits . . . I've seen people go into victim mode. "I'm not getting enough coaching, I'm not getting enough training."

. . . My history has been that I've worked in small companies that have grown quite large, so I had to be proactive about my training and learning. I was the one that reached out to my manager and said, "I need an hour of your time."

... When I got into this business, I had to have coaching sessions at 8:30 in the evening, because the gentleman I was working for [only had time then]. Thank goodness he gave me the time. Thank goodness I took the time at 8:30 in the evening to write down all the screw-ups I had made that day and then I'd say, "What should I have said?" Then I'd write down what I should have said. He was a great coach, but I was a great coachee.

Episode 249, July 7, 2020

Jane Gentry agrees that you should be proactive and not wait for others to make you better. You must make yourself better through reading, listening to podcasts, talking with colleagues, meeting with coaches, and more:

The one piece of advice that I would have for salespeople is, don't wait for somebody else to make you better.

The likelihood of your managers spending the time and the money to make you better is slim. Your company might try to make you better, but you own your success.

If you need to find a place like the Sales Institute or if you need to spend the money to find a coach to make you better at what you do, [then do that]. You need to be reading. You need to own your path in your career in sales.

Don't sit back and wait for somebody to make you a great salesperson.

Episode 132, March 11, 2019

By default, being coached or mentored means you'll continue to learn and grow. You can reach the outcomes you want and avoid any dreaded plateau.

Gene Zannetti is a motivational leader:

You have to trust the process. That's why you need a mentor. That's why you need to continue being a lifelong learner . . . If you don't do that, you'll never grow, you'll never have those outcomes you want. You'll plateau. . . .

I find salespeople and entrepreneurs generally make the best mentors, because they're always willing to pay it forward and to give back.

I guess what I'm trying to say here is that you know how many seeds are in an apple, but you never know how many apples are in a seed. Think about that. You don't know how many apples one seed can produce. You could count the number of seeds that are in an apple.

Plant seeds. Be a person of integrity. Give a lot of value. Don't expect anything in return. Have that integrity. Say what you mean, mean what you say, and good things tend to happen."

Episode 286, November 2, 2020

> ## "Don't wait for somebody else to make you better."
>
> *—Jane Gentry*
> *Episode 132, March 11, 2019*

Constructive feedback from a mentor can be helpful at any stage of your career. **Telesa Via** has found that those starting out in sales often want to hear about what a good job they're doing. That's understandable, yet cheerleading without any constructive wisdom won't be useful:

Find someone that you can connect with that is always going to do a reality check and provide you with a different way of looking at things, because the one way is not always the best way. . . . Always continue to find avenues to advance your learning.

Sometimes, in a professional setting, they may have areas of training . . . but not all sales companies offer that, so I would just say push yourself.

Go out and reach out to see what tools are out there to educate yourself on how to continue to sharpen your saw, because you cannot rely 100 percent on the company that you work with as the only way.

Episode 020, November 26, 2017

CHAPTER 10:
An Optimal Sales Mindset Is a Must

"[When it comes to mindset,] I go into every conversation with a client or a prospective client knowing—not thinking, not believing, but knowing—that no one is going to give them a better result and a better outcome than I am. I'm happy to serve. I'm happy to deliver those solutions to the client . . ."

—*Phil Curran*
Episode 129, February 27, 2019

Questions to Ponder:
- *Do you have the right mindset for sales success?*
- *How well do you handle objections and obstacles?*
- *Can you shift into a more powerful mindset as needed?*

Before the pandemic began, we would cover topics related to mindset about once a year. When the pandemic kicked in, we started doing a show every single week as a way of supporting sales professionals during a challenging time.

With the right mindset, you're courageous enough to understand that you're bringing customers value through the products and services that you offer. With the right mindset, you know you're going to be successful no matter what you do. You may not be successful every minute, but overall, you'll achieve success because you're focusing on what's helping your customer reach their goals.

Mindset isn't just confidence, by the way. Mindset is the ability to put yourself in a position where you know that you are bringing value to customers and that you are courageous enough to speak at the level of your customer.

Anyone with a desire to improve their mindset can do so. If you feel resistant to it, it'll be harder to expand and improve your mindset.

Adam Stalmack leads mortgage sales teams:

> You can teach mindset to the mind that's open to it. . . . It's developed over time. Some people will get it early on in life [and others] later in life, but where you're focused determines your reality.
>
> If you put a focus on that mindset, it can absolutely be developed and it can be taught over time.
>
> *Episode 205, February 3, 2020*

Mindset, combined with a decision to constantly learn, benefits you. When you add in good consultative skills and emotional intelligence, you form strong relationships.

Vaneet Bhaskar is a tech sales leader:

> You have to have a growth mindset. What I mean by that is, you have to constantly be learning in this space. I do it every day—learning something new every single day. That's the pace at which change is happening in this environment.
>
> *Episode 362, May 13, 2021*

Top sales speaker **Ron Karr** uses the acronym MAD to describe how mindset works in sales and life, and says our limiting beliefs and stories can negatively impact us:

> Let's talk about mindset. . . . **M**indset, **A**lignment and **D**estiny—the acronym is MAD. I want you to get MAD about your life. I want you to get MAD about where you want to be, but in a good way. . . .
>
> Mindset . . . dictates everything we do. It's how you're thinking. It's what you think is possible. It incorporates everything that's in your mind whether it's your aspirations, your fears, your stories, whatever. The one thing that can negatively impact our mindset is our limiting thoughts and beliefs—our stories.
>
> *Episode 391, August 10, 2021*

Writing can help you improve your mindset. You can journal or take notes to write about your goals as though they've already happened. That process encourages us to keep going and realize the goals.

Collin Mitchell is a sales podcaster:

> Write . . . things down as if they already happened and then sit with it and feel what the emotions are of achieving that. That's what's going to drive you forward to actually achieving those things. . . .
>
> [For my meditation practice,] I thought that I had to be this super Zen person and sit for twenty or thirty minutes in the morning . . . If you're running a little behind, it's hard to commit to sitting for twenty or thirty minutes.
>
> I've changed that to where I do five or ten minutes in the morning and then I meditate throughout the day . . . Because to take something that you do [like meditation] early in the morning and expect that's going to be sustainable for you to stay in that positive mindset [the entire day] to crush your goals is unrealistic.
>
> *Episode 399, August 31, 2021*

I discovered **David Morelli** when he hosted the very popular *Everything Is Energy* podcast.

He suggested that you can also write down all the ways you're feeling with the goal of improving your outcomes. Morelli says that it's only when you become authentic about how you're feeling that you can change and improve upon it or better understand your customer's mindset:

> The first thing to do is to write down all the ways that you're feeling, because once you acknowledge that and become authentic to that, you can switch into somebody else's mindset.
>
> I was coaching a C-suite person the other day and I said, "What do you think this other person that you're trying to have a good relationship with thinks?"
>
> They basically said all the things that they were thinking and feeling—*their* perspective. . . . I was like, that's good. Now let's put yourself in their mindset. . . . What's on the head of sales' mind right now? . . . Imagine being in their shoes, walking around.

Morelli notes that, in general, they're thinking about how to make another sale. After that work, they moved into what the person would be thinking about with regards to their personal life, such as what to do with their young children during a pandemic.

Part of the re-deployment of sales resources has been, "Go build relationships with your prospects . . . go have friendly calls. Because, when it's time for them to actually have budget and things, you're going to be the first person [they contact] because you cared about them as a person.

Episode 256, July 27, 2020

Elite salespeople approach sales as problem solvers—not as salespeople. The type of mindset you bring into relationships with customers affects the outcome.

John Asher:

Average salespeople are passive listeners—not very good at all. And to most buyers, they come across as having "commission breath," meaning, the buyer knows they're just there for their commission.

The elite salespeople have this whole different mindset, and that is, "I'm not a salesperson. I'm a problem solver." When you have that mindset, the buyers can sense it.

Episode 404, September 9, 2021

Alice Heiman adds that feeling grateful to have a conversation with someone creates a positive environment for conversations. She says this starts with your own mindset:

It starts with your own mindset. If I believe that someone's going to talk to me and be grateful to have that conversation, because I'm going to bring so much value to it, then I'm going to be able to have a wonderful conversation."

Episode 295, November 23, 2020

What's important in order to have a mindset that works for sales? Agility and a growth mindset contribute to the ability to keep going and trying new approaches. The ability to know you can learn and grow puts you at an advantage.

Amy Franko:

I see agility at the core as a growth mindset. . . .

Carol Dweck is the researcher who's probably most known in

that space [related to growth mindsets], although there are other researchers as well. The idea behind growth mindset is that, at your core, you see yourself as someone who has the ability to build capabilities and skills . . . You have the ability to expand and grow your skill set and, when you see yourself in that way, you are more willing to work on building skills. You are more willing to bring fresh ideas to a customer or prospect even if they aren't totally vetted.

You are more willing to take strategic risks and put yourself out there. As an individual seller assessing yourself on that spectrum, we all have some growth mindset. We all have some fixed mindset or, if you're a sales leader, thinking about your team: Who on your team has that growth mindset? . . . Who on your team might trend more toward a fixed mindset?

We have all of that inside our minds, but it's figuring out where we are on that spectrum and wanting to move ourselves more toward that growth mindset. . . . If we're going to build sales agility, we need to be conscious of building that growth mindset.

Episode 283, October 26, 2020

Your mindset will affect what you say in your calls—and it can either help or hinder you.

Andy Miller:

The mindset predetermines the outcome before you even begin. So if you think that picking up the phone and doing cold calling—and yes, people still cold call and yes, cold calling still works—[and] if you think nobody wants to talk to you, then you're going to act that way. Your words are going to come across that way.

If you think people do want to talk to you, then that matters, too. . . . I can't tell you which mindset is right or wrong, but [I can tell you] which mindset serves me better.

Episode 210, February 20, 2020

Nimit Bhatt shares precise steps for making those calls and suggests a "call-first" mindset:

[Try] incorporating a call-first mindset and more phone touches into your cadence. I've always been a big believer that the first step of any outbound cadence has to be a phone call. Phone call, leave a voicemail, and then send an email, in that order.

Episode 272, September 22, 2020

Part of that feeling of whether people want to talk to you or not can come from knowing and feeling that what you have is valuable and that the people you're calling need it.

Art Sobczak helps companies with sales prospecting:

You need to feel like what you have is so valuable—and again, assuming you're calling the right people—that everybody should have a need for it.

This doesn't mean that your messaging should say everyone needs what you're selling, but you do have to have that mindset when approaching calls.

Episode 312, January 11, 2021

> **"Mindset is so important in sales—not just today. Always. If you believe you can't sell today, you're right. If you believe you can sell today, you're right, and you get to choose what you're going to believe."**
>
> —*Lee Salz*
> *Episode 233, May 11, 2020*

Mindset is big money if you do the calculations. Sales leaders with the right mindset sell more. **Jamie Crosbie** is a well-known sales mindset trainer:

[We care about mindset because] sales leaders with a high-performing mindset sell 38 percent more. And it's no accident at all that, when we are able to master our mindset, we have more success and productivity. We have to understand what we're up against, especially at a time like this where we have a pandemic in place.

The National Science Foundation shows that we have 60,000 thoughts a day and, naturally, 80 percent of them are negative, which is astounding.... To take that one step further, during a crisis such as we're experiencing, we have to be even more thoughtful about overcoming those negative thoughts and learning how to flip the script.

Episode 305, December 20, 2020

Many of our guests recommend reading in order to improve your mind and to keep growing. While you can read and read, it's taking action with the knowledge gained that will help you. Try this actionable advice from **Alan Stein Jr.:**

If your performance, your mindset, and your productivity ebbs and flows with how you're feeling on any given day, then you'll never be a high performer, and you lack that portion of mindset.

When the world's spiraling out of control and you feel like you don't have control of anything, put your entire focus on the two things you do have control over, which is your own effort and your own attitude. . . .

We can't control the breaking news that's going to hit tomorrow, but all of us have control over the way that we will respond to it.

Take a breath. Take a beat. Respond in a way that's favorable. Know that your emotions are going to be on a roller coaster for the next several months, and that's okay. But don't let your behavior, your performance, or your mindset be dictated by them.

Episode 248, July 1, 2020

To create a growth mindset and to be creative, you have to be in a good place mentally. That begins with health.

Andy Miller:

When it comes to health, the biggest thing you can do for your immune system is [get] seven to eight hours of sleep . . . your body starts producing things that fight a disease at the seven-hour mark. Also . . . your brain actually relaxes and the little channels between different parts of your brain takes out the dead cells, so it's like the trash collector coming along to take out the trash. That immune-fighting ability and the brain taking away the trash through the spinal fluid does not happen until the seven-hour mark, so you need to get sleep.

Exercise. Somehow, when you're stressed, there are stress chemicals running throughout your body, [and] exercise burns them off . . . The body needs movement . . .

A bit of meditation every day . . . I do thirty minutes of meditation every day first thing in the morning, and part of my meditation is being thankful for what I have and where I'm at. No matter how bad things get, there's always something to be thankful for, and you're going to find you can be more creative.

Diet. Garbage in, garbage out . . .

The last thing is drinking and sugar. Alcohol and sugar [negatively] impact your immune system . . . it's not a value judgment conversation, but there are things that you can do to put yourself in a good place.

Episode 223, April 15, 2020

CHAPTER 11:
Sales Prospecting Is Easier When You Apply These Ideas

Questions to Ponder:
- *How comfortable are you picking up the phone to ask a prospect for a conversation?*
- *Do you experience call reluctance?*
- *Do you get joy when you finally get a prospect on the line?*

Frequently, sales professionals say prospecting is the most difficult stage of the sales process. During our shows and events, this was one of the hard skills that we focused on the most. This includes building your lists, understanding what to say, when to call, how to interact, when to use email versus voicemail or phone calls versus text.

As the customer becomes more knowledgeable about what they need and what your company brings to the marketplace, the whole process of prospecting changes to adapting to that. As we've addressed in previous chapters, the amount of value you bring must increase. Prospects are not interested in speaking with you, but if you help them identify blocks or things in the way of their success, you can become a valuable resource.

Prospecting is not for everybody in sales, so it's sometimes outsourced to SDRs (Sales Development Reps) and BDRs (Business Development Reps). Other times, companies hire junior sales professionals to make those initial calls and to get appointments for senior sales reps.

Not everyone excels at prospecting. Even senior sales leaders who enjoy prospecting don't seek to do it all the time. Getting somebody on the phone and engaging them in how you can be providing them solutions is the hardest part of sales. What follows is what sales professionals have found useful in their prospecting efforts.

Elite sales leaders say that persistence pays off. Sales prospecting expert **Caryn Kopp** includes persistence in the "3 Ps" she uses to talk about prospecting with others. They give you a simple way to remember what to do:

> There are the "3 Ps" of prospect follow-up that I talk about, which is: **P**ersistence with **P**atience without being a **P**est. You have to have those three.

> One of our clients was telling us her sales guy was not getting in enough doors, and we started looking at his activity . . . [Well,] he called one prospect twenty times in a week. Don't do that! Yes, the phone works, but not like that!

> *Episode 332, March 1, 2021*

With persistence and the right list, consistent prospecting can help you find the person who needs what you sell.

Bob Gilbert runs the Hospitality Sales and Marketing Association International:

> I believe that prospecting is ultimately the key attribute that will keep anybody moving forward and being successful. There is a customer for everything and for everybody.

> It's just a matter of if you have the right prospect list, and you're persistent about prospecting the right list, [then] you will find the right customer for whatever it is . . . you're selling. That's where that persistence and that questioning come into play from my perspective. If you think it's hard, it is hard, but that prospecting is what will differentiate you from the pack in terms of all your other peers out there . . .

> *Episode 208, February 13, 2020*

When it comes to persistence, you don't want to do too much and become a pest, and you also don't want to fall short. A study shares that the simple act of asking for something (a referral, the business, an introduction) more than five times can improve your results.

Andy Miller:

> [You may be] familiar with the Chicken Soup for the Soul series that was done by Jack Canfield and Mark Victor Hansen . . . These

guys were sales trainers before they did the Chicken Soup for the Soul series, and they did a study on salespeople and how often salespeople . . . were people asking for what they wanted. In this case, I'm saying you're asking for the deal . . . [an introduction, a referral, a conversation with the decision committee].

Here's what they found out:

- 54 percent of salespeople never asked [for anything].
- Only 46 percent asked one time.
- 24 percent asked twice.
- 14 percent asked three times.
- 12 percent asked four times.
- Only 4 percent asked five times.

The crazy thing is 60 percent of all deals are closed after asking five times. That means you've got to ask six times or more.

How many of us have stopped short?

Episode 309, January 4, 2021

To keep from feeling discouraged, remember that every "no" you hear means you're a step closer to a "yes."

Lisa Peskin is the founder of the Business Development University:

Think about it like this: If you're prospecting, think about the world as a finite jar of black-and-white jelly beans. Every black one is a "no" and every white one is a "yes." So if you're prospecting, you need to pick out so many black ones before you can get to the white ones.

Every time you get a no, say, "This is good, because it's bringing me closer to the white one." And, again, it's all about the way we look at things . . . Do we want to go through life looking at all the negatives . . . or do we want to find the good in everything because there is so much good?

. . . The next piece is, we've got to build that pipeline with good, qualified prospects on a consistent basis, and all of you might be saying, ". . . How do I get those new prospects in my pipeline?"

You've got to take a multipronged approach . . . If you're not using video in your prospecting, you might want to start doing that.

I had a guy from Israel send me a personalized video. [When we spoke], he asked, "Why did you take my meeting?" I said, "Because you made a personalized video for me."

Pick up the phone. The phone is ten times more effective than emails . . . You can use letters. All these things are going to differentiate you from other people.

. . . One of my clients used the 'Info@' [email] on somebody's website and got into a large shark tank company . . . We try different things. Not everything works for everybody. Not everything works in every situation.

Make sure that you're motivated enough not only to pick up that phone but to have a cadence hitting so many heavy-hitter prospects on a consistent basis with a multitouch program. If you don't have a program [consisting of] eight to twelve touches, you're not going to get in the door with as many net new prospects, and [doing] that is one of the keys to your success.

When that pipeline is full, we stop pushing and then we get that confidence.

Episode 308, December 29, 2020

To handle prospecting requires a thick skin, because you'll be told "no" often. Prospecting is always a key to making things happen.

Joe Alvarez is a leading businessman in the office space industry. As he says below, you can't sell if you don't have enough activity:

It's very evident that you've got to have thick skin, because you get told "no" a lot, and it never bothered me, because I think one of the assets that I have is, I don't take it personally.

When somebody says no, it's not about me. It's about my product, my service, or perhaps they're having a bad day . . .

One of the things that I learned from that was, prospecting was a key to making things happen.

[If] you don't have enough activity, you can't sell.

Episode 037, January 24, 2018

Handwritten and interesting cards sent by mail help keep you top of mind.

Alice Heiman:

I have been sending these cards to my clients and prospects for years and sometimes, when I go visit them three years later, I still see the card pinned to their board, because it's a photograph on a beautiful piece of paper, and I write a note.

What do I write inside these notes? Sometimes, I write "congratulations," because I watch the news, and I see that they won [an award for] "best places to work" or that they've just changed jobs or something else unusual that I find on LinkedIn or by doing a Google Alert.

I'm constantly watching my clients and prospects, so I send a card [when I see something to celebrate]. You might say, "Alice, I don't have their address and nobody's in their office." That's fine. Maybe that's one you can't do right at this minute if you don't have their address [and you do it later].

Episode 295, November 23, 2020

When it comes to social selling, read on for suggestions on how to approach people and what research you can do via social media before calls.

Janet Schijns:

Social selling is about one-to-one [and] one-to-few. You're trying to build—just like you would in any other sales setting—an authentic, genuine, real relationship that takes a connection to a prospect into sales and revenue.

Social marketing—putting things on your company's page or posting about your company—that's one-to-many, and your goal there is to just extend your brand awareness to a broad array of connections and influencers, including the people you went to college with, people you worked with at your last job, and maybe a prospect. . . .

Social selling is critical to your sales success. . . . When you social sell, it's all about . . . how recently has the prospect heard your voice? How frequently do you engage with them?

[On] the movement of the prospect: How is the relationship moving forward? How are you doing the things that are going to take this from a connection to a relationship [and] from a relationship to a sale?

Episode 360, May 10, 2021

In another chapter, we shared ways to research. Research and prospecting go hand in hand, and the availability of information through social media makes the process simpler than in the past.

Brynne Tillman is known as "The LinkedIn Whisperer":

> One of the things that we've learned with social [media] is, we can learn so much about our prospects before our meeting that we should go [into the meeting] ... knowing much more than they'd expect us to know ...
>
> [For example, we can ask a specific question]: "I noticed a press release that your company put out about three weeks ago around X. How is that affecting you?"
>
> Then they think, "They did their homework ..."
>
> There's a little secret hack that I do [on LinkedIn] if I'm looking at a prospect, [such as] a big company I'm trying to get into. I'll do a search for people that were in similar roles to the person that I'm meeting with at that company. You can search [for] past roles at past companies, so I can connect with folks. [For example,] maybe I'm looking to speak with the VP of Sales at ABC Company. I can search who used to be at ABC Company as the VP of Sales and reach out to them, and I can get a ton of insights from former employees.
>
> *Episode 154, May 27, 2019*

Obsess over people and your process, and it could take you far in your career, as it has for **Carson Heady**, author of *Salesman on Fire*:

> Think about where your audience is. Be there, [and] use the tools that are going to get you there.
>
> Create relationships. Try to do it at a high frequency ...
>
> Be consistent. Make sure that you actually have a consistent approach, because prospecting is not something you just do in the first quarter. It's something you're doing constantly, because if your pipeline dries up and you have nothing to put back in its place, then you're leaving yourself high and dry.
>
> You want to constantly be making deposits into that prospecting funnel and creating new conversations and relationships.
>
> Over time, if you effectively bring your resources to bear with all these wonderful new people that you're meeting, you give yourself the best probability of success.

. . . I've never had to worry about my results. I've obsessed over people and process, and that has taken care of me for an entire career.

Episode 349, April 8, 2021

Make the calls before working on proposals.

Howard Langsam is a sales and business leader:

Make those calls. . . . If you don't get your prospecting over in the morning or set time of the day, you'll get all the way to the end of the day having worked on proposals all day . . . [If] your prospecting time got crowded out . . . you go a quarter later and your pipeline is empty. . . . it's way too easy to do the in-front-of-you work of writing proposals and qualifying leads, but you must force yourself [to make the calls].

After you close the deals that are closable that day, go right to the top of the funnel and work from the top down so that you're not having a famine next quarter.

Episode 290, November 12, 2020

If you're afraid to prospect, take a deeper look at what might be causing the feeling to show up.

Klyn Elsbury is a motivational keynote speaker and wellness expert:

When you tell me that you are afraid of prospecting calls or you have a fear of picking up the phone, I'm sure you do. I'm not discrediting that and, if you go deeper, is it the fear of the rejection of when you pick up the phone?

. . . Address what it is that's going on that's making you afraid to prospect, because you're either at the core of it feeling like you're not enough or you're not loved . . . [And you might worry] if you don't do it correctly, that you will experience less—less income, less territory, less responsibilities, less abundance in the world. [Or you worry] you will experience loss and, by loss, that means your job could be completely eliminated, the product line is completely eliminated . . .

Breathe through your nose, exhale through [your] mouth, and simply ask yourself, "Which fear is being lit up for me right now?" . . . That's when we start to lean into how to address the issue.

Episode 258, August 5, 2020

Take into account when you'll have the best chance of reaching your prospects.

Lee Salz:

> You want to prospect outside the business [times] 7:30 a.m. to 9:00 a.m. in the time [zones] where they are, and 5:00 p.m. to 6:00 p.m. in the time [zones] where they are, to increase your hit rate of connecting with them. . . .
>
> [On another note, one] of the fears that executives have is not having enough time for a proper implementation—that you're going to disrupt some business flow [with your product or service] . . . we have to guide them to recognize that they have this opportunity right now for proper consideration of what an alternative solution could look like and proper planning around implementation."
>
> *Episode 233, May 11, 2020*

Write down how your solution has helped others. You'll clarify the benefits of your solution and be more prepared with an effective success story to share during conversations.

Nimit Bhatt:

> Take the action item of actually writing out in your own words how your solution has helped . . . [a customer or prospect, and] talk about how you've actually solved a certain problem for a prospect before . . .
>
> If you sell a solution that has multiple use cases, come up with one for each use case and then next time you're on a call, I suggest calling your hardest prospect or calling somebody that maybe you called three weeks ago. They're not going to remember you. Try to get curious with them. Lead them to one of those use cases, [and] then tell that story and see if that can get you farther into the process.
>
> *Episode 272, September 22, 2020*

Give your prospects permission to tell you no.

Will Fuentes is a top sales trainer in the Washington, DC, region:

> A prospect [usually] doesn't want to let that salesperson down so, as a salesperson, we have to give them permission to tell us no. We

have to let them know that it's okay for them to say [that]. . . .

Right now, [with prospecting], empathy becomes . . . [important] on both sides, and we have to tell people [on our team] that honesty is more important [than merely pushing people to a yes].

. . . One of the things that I tell salespeople today is, ask your prospect to turn on their camera. . . . Here's why. If they say to me, "My kids are running around, and I don't feel comfortable," you say, "No problem . . ."

Now, you also know that they're probably going to be distracted during that call. Your empathetic moment, which is also a sales moment, allows you to come back and say, "If you've got to take care of your kids, maybe we can reschedule. I'm happy to do that. I'll provide some times for you . . ."

If they say, "No, I'm good," you now have permission to move off of empathy into sales mode, because they are telling you, "I am ready to listen to what you have to say."

Episode 259, August 6, 2020

CHAPTER 12:
Top Sales Professionals Have Indispensable Relationships That Pay Off for Decades

"Relationships are not between logos or buildings. They're always between individuals—individuals, teams, and organizations . . ."

—*David Nour*
Episode 213, March 10, 2020

Questions to Ponder:
- *Do you expect something in return from all your relationships?*
- *Are you a giver versus a taker?*
- *Do you like to connect people, even if there's no direct benefit to you in the short run?*

When *The Challenger Sale* came out, relationships got a bad rap. At that time, a lot of sales professionals believed that they were skilled and successful in sales because they had developed relationships over years. Then, *Challenger* said education and insight were more critical.

Well, relationships are critical for a couple of different reasons. People do like to buy from people that they like and trust, and people like long-term relationships. We've had some guests on the *Sales Game Changers Podcast* who have been with their company for decades. In some cases, they've spent twenty to thirty years at the same company and, because of the nature of their customer—be it government or financial services or banking—their customer has been a customer for the same amount of time. In many cases, the relationships moved beyond business to become friendships.

> "The customer is not a customer today or for a month or for a year . . . It's a lifelong commitment, and all of the efforts that you do day in and day out should reflect that."
>
> —*Brian Green*
> *Episode 001, October 9, 2017*

Sales leaders we've interviewed usually can point to people they've worked with for twenty to thirty years. Maybe they worked together at a company and then they went separate ways, and then maybe came back together as companies were acquired and merged. The critical nature of the business relationship is that, especially when an emergency like a pandemic happens, people would break through the barriers of business and begin talking about what's happening personally—not just in business. Everybody has been affected by the pandemic on both business and personal levels.

The ability to speak to people can also lead to enjoyment in the job. We may not always talk about the fact we can have fun and deeply enjoy our work in sales. Most people enjoy sales when they're successful, because it's afforded them great lives. It's afforded them the ability to buy a nice house and cars and use their money for things that they want to use it for, such as vacations, hobbies, boats, and more. But it's the relationships that allow them to continue, and the reason these long-term relationships continue to develop is because value is shared on both sides.

Melissa Riley is a leader in the hospitality, convention, and travel industries:

> At the end of the day, sales is about relationships, and some of my best days in the office are when you have a bid that you've been working on for some time—years—and that signature finally comes through on the dotted line. There's nothing more exceptional than ringing that bell and all celebrating together.
>
> I say sales isn't hard, and some of that stems from the fact that I do love what I do, and I sell a city that I absolutely love . . . [When I attended a conference] in Barcelona, Spain . . . my colleague and I were sitting

at an outdoor cafe for dinner, and we struck up a conversation with the couple that were sitting next to us. . . . Come to find out, they're coming to Washington [which is the city I promote].

Since then . . . [the woman in the couple] and I have become best friends via email. I've sent her tickets to things that she needs to do and see in the city [and] offered her my best suggestions on restaurants . . . This isn't my core job responsibility, but at the end of the day, it's my job to be an ambassador for the city [of Washington, DC]. So, whether it's wooing 40,000 people for a large conference coming to the center or making sure that . . . [a couple from Scotland has] an incredible experience and makes some great memories here in Washington, DC, that's my job, and that's why I love sales.

Episode 069, May 2, 2018

Cultivate your network and know that the relationships you're building are for the long term.

Patrick Narus:

It comes down to networking and relationships. Network your butt off. Meet folks. Offer yourself as a service to others.

You don't want to ever be perceived as taking [or] needing. Offer something in return, but it genuinely all boils down to relationships and referrals.

Cultivate that networking aspect of your life . . .

Episode 393, August 12, 2021

When it comes to sales, price is not the issue. The customer needs to understand the value, and you need to have a good relationship with the customer.

Use outreach methods to start building relationships. You can read through the chapter on prospecting to get more ideas for how to approach relationship development.

Carson Heady:

Sales is relationships and probability. If I reach out to more people than anybody else and I do it with the right messaging, I have a higher probability of getting those meetings. And if I can't get the

CEO or the CFO meeting right out of the gate, I'll swarm. I'll reach out to every influencer in that relationship and eventually . . . I'll get to the person that I want.

But it's all about adding value and understanding that element.

So how did I become the top social seller? By practicing what I believed to be the right mechanisms, by evolving [my] approach based on results and sometimes lack thereof, and, ultimately, by creating meaningful relationships.

Social opens the door, but what you do with it once you're in the door is what's going to determine your success. That's it. It's fine to get a meeting, but if you don't actually do something to stay top of mind after the fact, then you're not going to be able to maintain those relationships.

Episode 349, April 8, 2021

When you do that outreach, don't rush it. Take the time to learn the details.

Caryn Kopp:

Some tips for you: Close your phone, don't look at your phone, don't look at your texts, don't look at anything. Just focus on the individuals who you've identified as the people who need you, who feel urgency, who would willingly pay, who would find you to be an obvious solution, and [then] open up a relationship with them.

. . . If you do your research and tell them why this meeting is so important to them, that's a whole different ballgame in terms of creating a relationship. Having the right door opener do the right kind of work is one of the most efficient ways of developing new business and being successful."

Episode 332, March 1, 2021

What follows are tips to establish long-term relationships.

David Nour talked about how there are fundamental laws in relationships:

- No. 1 is gratitude. Say thank you.
- No. 2 is reciprocity. If someone isn't asking how they can help you, your spidey sense should go up.
- No. 3 is pay it forward.

. . . If I continue to invest [in a relationship], and I'm not seeing those fundamental laws—gratitude, reciprocity, pay it forward—I'm always nice and take the high road, but I get a chance to deprioritize someone and prioritize somebody else on that list.

Episode 213, March 10, 2020

As you establish long-term relationships, you'll receive referrals. They're a big compliment from your past customers. Long-term relationships help you increase the number of referrals you receive.

Ivy Savoy-Smith:

I'm here to build relationships. I'm here to build long relationships and the biggest compliment in sales is a referral to me.

To be able to get a referral from a client speaks volumes, because that just shows how much they trust you to then refer you to one of their friends for business.

When I started getting referrals I was like, "Now you're onto something, Ivy, keep doing what you're doing."

It's just being fair and honest and doing what you say you're going to do, executing when you say you are, and, if something goes wrong, be upfront about it. Be proactive. Don't wait. Don't react. Be proactive. That has helped me in my career go a lot further than even I thought I would at this time.

Episode 142, April 15, 2019

Let people know you'll be there for them in good times or bad.

Dave Rey was the Institute for Excellence in Sales Lifetime Award recipient in 2022:

People buy from people they like and trust and this, to me, has been the foundation for a long-term relationship with your customers.

[Secondly,] learn and appreciate the task or mission of your customer that you're solving for. Let the people know that you're going to be there in the good times and the difficult times and that will, over time, build the trust that you need to have a long-term relationship with your customers.

Episode 087, July 24, 2018

As you move into management, strive to keep in touch with the concerns of your market.

Dorean Kass played in the Rose Bowl for Stanford and took his lessons from the gridiron into the boardroom:

> What makes sales leaders and salespeople in general successful is their ability to build relationships and drive value for their customers.
>
> As you move into sales management, you get further and further away from the customer. It disintermediates your ability to know what's going on directly . . . It's something that you have to strive to maintain, because it keeps you effective in knowing what is truly relevant for your clients, and it gives you the opportunity to build relationships with your sales team to understand how are they positioning things and what's the response in the room, [which are] things that you can't learn just from debriefing after the fact.

Episode 034, January 17, 2018

Success in sales is defined as being good at "the inches" around you. In other words, focus on small successes or elements just as you would big successes or elements. Also, as you enter management, remember that it's important to build relationships with your own people. One way to do that is to be the first to celebrate even the small wins of your team.

Mark Cerminaro:

> One of the things that is extremely important as you get into sales leadership is to build relationships with your people.
>
> You have to build trust . . . they have to look to you to [as] somebody that, when you're being constructive, they genuinely believe it to be constructive feedback to help benefit them or else they tend to not fully engage in what you're saying.
>
> You have to be the first person to congratulate them when something is good. Not just big successes, but little successes . . . I've always been a fan of quoting a scene from *Any Given Sunday*, a movie with Al Pacino, where he talks about [how] the inches are everywhere . . . In the world of sales, success is defined by being good at the inches around you. It's not just the big things, but it's the inches around you that help you be successful in perfecting those.

Episode 032, January 10, 2018

The one-to-one relationship is critical, and you can establish that in numerous ways that relate to your business or company.

Jim Van Stone:

> People buy from people they like . . . [who] respect and . . . understand what their objectives and goals are. That one-on-one relationship is absolutely critical, and when you look at our facility here at Capital One Arena, . . . for a given Capitals or Wizards game, someone could come down here and have a game-changing experience. They can see a Hall of Fame moment that happens, and that's a personal experience when you're there live and in person.
>
> For us, when we look at all of our guests and customers, and they're coming to see us, we take that very . . . [seriously], so getting out to meet as many customers as you can on a game night is important. . . .
>
> Relationships are valuable and the better relationships that we develop with our customers certainly can lead to high levels of retention.
>
> *Episode, 230, May 5, 2020*

When you get the story of your prospect correct, they appreciate it. Take on some of the habits of an investigative reporter to get the information you need to share the story in the proposal.

Eileen Kent is an expert on government contracting:

> In a way, salespeople are like investigative reporters, creating a strong relationship with the customer, getting the story, and bringing it back. Then, when we say "capture," we're capturing the story and then we're repeating it back to them in the proposal. And they go, "That's exactly what I wanted," because you got the [correct] story.
>
> *Episode 367, June 1, 2021*

Use social media. Even when challenges arise, you can find creative ways to build relationships.

Pramod Raheja:

> Own your own onboarding, absolutely. To add to that . . . we're trying to go after a certain type of business and, normally, you would have to get in front of a lot of people and, normally, we would get in front of a lot of people to get this business.

Unfortunately, that has not been possible at all, and we got this opportunity just as COVID hit, so everything's online.

I'm going to get a little more tactical in terms of what I'll say. LinkedIn has been an amazing tool. I always like to say, "If you're not LinkedIn, you're linked out."

All of sales is building relationships, so we've been building relationships using LinkedIn as a tool. So now, three months after COVID, I've got so many potential in-person happy hours with people across the country once we get past all of this, because of the relationships that are being built online . . .

Episode 254, July 20, 2020

Global sales leader **Randy Wood** suggested:

The biggest thing I learned that I carry with me every day is the importance of influence, because what you're trying to gain and earn with your customer is a level of influence. I want to influence my customer to take action or to do something different or to ultimately buy my product.

If you break down influence, a couple of things stand out—like what does influence mean? I want to be relevant. I need to bring a level of relevance to what I'm doing. I need to be competent and, most importantly, I need to be credible.

Episode 164, July 15, 2019

Be a friend to someone. Extending relationships beyond getting the sale can be rewarding personally.

Zeev Wexler is a social media marketing guru:

If you are able to be a friend to someone, if you are able to not just be there because of who you represent and the company that you work for, it creates amazing relationships. [With these people,] I know that I can pick up the phone and ask . . . for help that is not related to my business . . . You can't build those relationships just by talking about sales.

Episode 400, September 1, 2021

CHAPTER 13:
The Top Reps Prepare and Here's Why

"If you do your research and tell them why
this meeting is so important to them, that's a
whole different ballgame in terms of creating a
relationship. Having the right door opener do the
right kind of work is one of the most efficient ways
of developing new business and being successful."

—*Caryn Kopp*
Episode 332, March 1, 2021

Questions to Ponder:
- *How much time do you spend preparing for a sales call?*
- *How often do you wing it?*
- *Are you excited about knowing more about your prospect's business goals?*

The topic of preparation comes up when we ask sales leaders, "What should you be doing to be more successful?" One of our long-time guests, Steve Richard, has suggested a "three-by-three" process, which involves finding three things out about the customer in three minutes. John Asher, one of our sponsors, talks about the applied personality platform Crystal Knows, and about understanding personal elements about the customer before you engage.

> "Salespeople have to be fanatical about research. Number one: research the company and the competition. Number two: research the buyer themselves. Number three: go to Crystal Knows, so that you understand the buyer's personality style. So [that way], when you reach out to them, you're targeting exactly to their personality style. Find out everything you can about what's going on [and] what their needs are."
>
> —John Asher
> Episode 404, September 9, 2021

While we often talk about how you don't need to spend a huge amount of time to prepare for a call, we do advise that you learn your customer's challenges. You need to know what's going on in your customer's industry. There's no excuse for not doing that. Asking open-ended questions is great, but the questions can't be ignorant or you risk losing their trust. Customers are busy, especially if they hold a higher role in the organization, so you need to understand, in advance of any conversations, what they're going through.

It's not hard to do the research anymore. You can search Google and find anything about any industry, and you'll come up with dozens of things that are talked about, including news, regulations, or new developments.

Obviously, with the pandemic, we know what has happened to certain industries. We know what's happened to the entertainment industry, higher education, and, of course, health care. We know about the government shifting to the cloud quickly—and more quickly than we expected. There's no excuse for sales professionals to not know what is going on in their customer's marketplace and where it's heading. Elite sales professionals are the ones who know that and spend the time to understand and focus on it.

As we've talked about in other chapters, sales reps need to understand their customer's goals and expect changes.

Matt McDarby:

If we don't know what our clients or prospects are trying to achieve, this job is infinitely harder than when we do know that. That's my No. 1 expectation for my team.

This is about putting yourself in position to pivot, and the other bit of advice here is expecting the change. I've been doing this a long time and I can't think of a year where we've been able to fully execute the strategy that we anticipated executing on January 1. . . . It just doesn't work that way. As a sales leader you need to be prepared to pivot, and that may be one of the most important skills you can develop.

Episode 325, February 11, 2021

Be sure you do your research before you start asking questions.

Andrea Cohen:

Don't go in and start asking questions until you've actually done some thorough research on those customers.

Talk to other accounts, and talk to people that have other federal modules, and learn what the common problems are, because there are a number of common problems. [These include] aging infrastructure, ability to recruit new people . . . The other thing I would say is sit down and have coffee and go meet with your customers—not to try to sell them something—but to understand their business and what drives them. You don't get that [information] unless you're talking to them . . . [when] you're not trying to push a product.

Episode 160, June 24, 2019

Your research can lead you to discover common interests or shared backgrounds. For instance, you may follow the same sport, enjoy the same hobbies, or find you attended the same school.

Michelle Hecht is a successful sales trainer:

I do research on the people that I reach out to, and I look for a commonality that I might have with them—whether it's being a mom, being a wife, being in sales, [or] a specific industry. I'll take one or two little pearls that I have in common with them, and I will use a little humor, a little sarcasm [in an intro], but it's an intro and I'm not looking to sell anybody anything.

I just want to make a human connection with them first. If the conversation continues and it goes back and forth a couple of times, then I will talk to them about what I do. I'll ask them what they do, and I want to meet them where they're at.

Episode 282, October 26, 2020

While research is important, it's vital not to let it slow you down or paralyze you.

Brian Ludwig is a sales leader in the event software industry:

There's a part of me that says, "If you do too much research before a call, it's paralyzing."

I've seen too many reps stare at the screen for ten minutes before they make a phone call because they're doing all of the research. I want them to move fast. It's a double-edged sword.

I want the efficiency, but I want them to know enough to be dangerous . . . It is that balancing act that I want them at 80 percent comfort level over what's the value proposition, what's the story, who else have we worked with that's similar that we solved a similar pain [point for].

Episode 141, April 10, 2019

Formulate a game plan and strategy based on your research.

Gary Newgaard:

For people entering the sales arena, you have to formulate your game plan and your strategy based on your research of the customer and understanding what challenges they face. [For example,] not asking closed-end questions—yes/no questions—[but instead] getting the customer to expose to you what the problem is they're trying to solve. . . .

[I tell people this is like] the NFL, and you have to stay in shape, which means you have to understand what's going on in the market [and] be a student of the game. You have to do your homework and understand what your competition is doing, understand what your prospect or customer is trying to accomplish, and be that person that can earn a position of trust as opposed to [only] being [seen as] a salesperson.

Episode 052, March 9, 2018

Use your research to inform your introduction or conversation.

Christopher Ware:

Before I pick up the phone [or] before I send an email, I've done at least some base level research online and confirm that they are in fact a prime prospect.

Oftentimes . . . what I like to do is . . . [use] LinkedIn [and] basic Google searches. [For example,] you have a chance to read people's press releases [to learn more about what makes them proud and what they've accomplished].

Episode 071, May 8, 2018

Be sure to measure qualitatively and not just quantitatively when it comes to numbers of calls and other measured actions. When you focus on quality, preparation is part of that.

Craig Mueller:

Preparation is key. When I was at Linear, it was very metrics driven. Activity based meetings aren't the way to go, [because] then we're just measuring quantitative [metrics, such as] "ten calls a week." We need to . . . measure qualitatively. If we look at quality and we start to sit down, the first piece is preparation.

Episode 209, February 17, 2020

When it comes to preparation, focus on time and territory.

Tom Young has led sales teams in enterprise and information software:

I've literally seen over the years many times where I could almost track the success of a given individual to the time that they had spent in that territory. And I felt like a lot of times the effort the teams go through in changing their territories too frequently, too quickly, or dividing them into smaller units had a detrimental effect on performance.

Episode 066, April 20, 2018

CHAPTER 14:
Knowing How to Speak Your Value Proposition Is a Must

"The key to selling value is to be the value. In other words, you can't regurgitate what someone can find with two clicks on Google. They don't need you for that. They don't need you to talk about the product, the specifications, the prices. They need you to understand what's going on with them."

—*Dave Kurlan*
Episode 408, September 20, 2021

"[Value is about] building reputation in the marketplace."

—*Meridith Elliott Powell*
Episode 375, June 21, 2021

Questions to Ponder:
- *Are you comfortable speaking your company's value proposition in ways that resonate with your customer?*
- *Do you believe your company's value proposition?*
- *Have you considered ways to be creative speaking your company's value prop?*

In *SPIN Selling*, one of the classic sales books, Neil Rackham said that sales has always been about value creation. We know that the customers are not going to be spending their dollars if they can't see the value in what you're providing. Since the customer can find out what your product or service does without even talking to a sales rep, it's vital that sales professionals bring extreme value to the customer, both for what the customer needs to accomplish today and what the customer needs to accomplish with their customer—and their customer's customer—for the foreseeable future.

As we move forward, and industries shift and change, it's critical to understand and share the value you bring and to do so from the customer's perspective.

> ## "Clients never forget folks that can come to the table and add value to what they're trying to do."
> —*Tim Atkinson*
> *Episode 075, June 1, 2018*

If you're not hearing back from people, revisit what value you're bringing to the customer. Consider what you're contributing to their success and how you can be consultative in your approach.

Bob Stevens:

If you're not bringing value to the customer, then they're not going to see you. That's the bottom line.

I hear all too often a salesperson saying, "I've emailed and I called and I don't ever hear back from them."

Well, I wonder what your message is, because it's something that's not resonating. [If that's the case,] you might want to think about changing it in order to resonate and provide that value that they need.

Episode 102, October 11, 2018

The days of merely sharing benefits are over, so it's necessary to convey value to your customers and prospective customers.

Frank Cespedes is the author of *Sales Management That Works*:

The days of the salesperson essentially being an organic walking, talking version of direct mail are over. Because in most markets, especially B2B markets, the buyers already have product information, product comparisons, price comparisons.

Episode 350, April 12, 2021

Howard Brown:

I get hundreds of phone calls. It's nonstop. My time is incredibly valuable, as is all of ours. If you're going to reach out to me, you better deliver value and you better do it quickly, because if all I'm hearing is about you and your product, I'm done, I'm moving on. Those days are over.

Episode 344, March 29, 2021

Eric Trexler is a software sales leader:

You've got to provide value . . . If you're going to talk to a customer or prospect, you better understand what that value proposition is. You're sharing something somebody else in the industry is doing like them. You're bringing them something that you perceive to be of value.

. . . Saying, "Hey, I don't know you, but how can I help? What can I do for you?" [doesn't help]. I probably get five of those calls a day, and they're a total turnoff for me. I'll never do business with that company again . . . I need value and I need it now and so do our customers.

Episode 222, April 15, 2020

One way to share your value is before any sales conversations take place—through your content.

Anthony Robbins has led high-performing sales teams:

The customers care most about your understanding of the work that they do and how you might add value to the problems that they have or the business challenges they're trying to solve. So the best sales reps today have intimate knowledge of their customers and bring them compelling value where they educate or inspire them to do things differently or to do things better. That's the number one thing. The second thing that has to occur is, we have to digitally transform the profession of sales, largely driven, as I said earlier, by the fact that the customer's buying journey has forever and profoundly changed.

We've got to get our sales teams creating great content of value and creating virtual presence through social channels to meet their customers where they are and making sure that we add value to the business that they're in.

Episode 009, October 27, 2017

Sales development leader **Kevin Dorsey** shares questions that help you with both your content and the content of your discovery calls:

If you go ask [certain] questions of fifty customers, I promise you, your sales results will improve.

Because, why did they buy? There's your value prop.

What problems were they hoping to solve? There are your subject lines, your first sentences, your bullet points, and your discovery questions.

What were they afraid of before buying? There's your 8-Mile and your unspoken objections.

What are they not telling you in the sales process? What was the sales process? Now you know who you actually need to convince behind the scenes.

What's their favorite part? There are your values.

What do they love the most? Those are your case studies.

And how would they describe [the problems] is how you start to get yourself to speak their language.

Episode 359, May 6, 2021

Be specific as to what value you bring to the situation.

Shawn Cook has led numerous sales teams:

We're going to help you to avoid landmines. We're going to educate you on new issues and outcomes. If you decide to continue talking to us, we're going to help you to get widespread support within your organization, and we've created high-value meetings . . . that offer you the ability to choose an alternative ending . . . What you have to do now is make sure that you offer high-value meetings—

conversations that keep the conversation going and keep you moving to the next thing.

Episode 092, August 20, 2018

Amy Su:

We might think of it as the sale or the metric or the quota, all of which are important. But if we brought in that frame and said, "What am I actually contributing to my customers? What's the value add? How do I be consultative? How do I add value to their business or help them solve their problems?" Then we're expanding our sense of purpose even more.

Episode 394, August 17, 2021

When you have value and the customer has a need, you don't need to badger people.

Larry Levine is the author of *Selling from the Heart*:

The question that I'd like everybody to ask is: "What value have I been bringing to your organization?" And stop and listen. For many salespeople, that means you may have to bite your tongue so hard that it bleeds . . . I promise everybody this—this question will get you so many responses: "How can I be of service to you right now?" Listen.

Episode 338, March 15, 2021

Andy Miller:

If you're badgering [a prospect], don't badger. If you're desperate, don't beg. An ask is simply an ask. "Can I have some of your french fries? Can you buy me a coffee?" That's just an ask and they go, "Sure, I'll help you get a coffee" or "I'm happy sharing my french fries." That's not begging. But if you ask them twenty times, I would say you must look at what you're selling, who you're approaching, and do they need what you have? Because if they don't need what you have, there's no reason to ask six times. The answer is still going to be no.

Episode 309, January 4, 2021

Get clear on your message of value and how it can gain additional revenue for the organization.

Chris Cutino:

Value is in the eye of the beholder . . . what's the overall value for the organization? . . . We've had to pivot away from, "We can save you time, we can make you more efficient." We have to be able to show them that, "We can get you better results and ultimately you're going to gain additional revenue for your organization by using these tools."

Episode 056, March 16, 2018

Amy Franko is the author of *The Modern Seller*:

A modern seller is someone who is recognized as a differentiator in your client's business. . . . Marrying yourself to your product or service and the expertise that you bring as an individual seller amplifies the value of your product or service. It amplifies the value of your organization, so never underestimate yourself as a valuable part of that equation.

. . . Your clients view you as someone who is so strategic to their competitive advantage, they can't imagine not doing business with you. You are ingrained in their organization in a way that they couldn't separate themselves from you or your organization, because they just view you as so strategic. Do you have modern selling in your repertoire, or maybe there are some things to be working on?

Episode 283, October 26, 2020

Remember how and why partners were valuable to you. It's easy to forget, and forgetting can be costly.

Bethann Pepoli:

A lot of times in this job you're consistently trying to prove yourself. There are a lot of sales reps that say, "I don't think this partner is bringing any value . . . " That's where a lot of the refereeing and executive sponsorship comes into place, and you're fighting about, "Let's go back a year and remember they ran a workshop. They invested in training for the customer. They did all of these things along the way to help get this deal to the finish line, which is where you are today."

Talking directly with customers and prospects about why they didn't see value can give you valuable information to improve your results.

Episode 311, January 10, 2021

Caroline Tuner mentions the benefit of listening to "unhappy client" feedback calls.

Caroline Turner:

One of the things that I enjoy doing is being on those unhappy client feedback calls. So, you know, under customer success, you're going to have people that are unhappy with your product. They're going to drop and that feedback is so invaluable when somebody is willing to take the time in telling you why they didn't see value.

Episode 003, October 13, 2017

Your silence is just as important as asking the questions in the first place.

Tonya Bjurstrom:

"What value do we bring to you?" That is a great question. It's very open-ended. It gives the customer lots of opportunity to answer in whatever way they think is most appropriate.

. . . You need to allow that silence, even if it becomes an awkward silence, to give that customer time to process what kind of answers they want to provide.

Episode 372, June 15, 2021

Start with your customer in the center and work backwards, as **Carrie-Anne Mosley** suggests:

If you start with the customer in the center and work backwards in your sales strategy development, you're going to be much more successful.

How can you get to know your customer . . . [and] your customer's customer, and then realize what value, whatever you're selling, has to both of those? Then, articulate that to the customer throughout the sale cycle. That will help you help your customer to make an internal business case to buy your solution.

Episode 189, October 29, 2019

Think beyond instant gratification to the longer-term results and success.

Chris Townsend leads successful tech sales teams:

> "Trusted adviser" is an overused term, but it's about understanding how to add value beyond the sale. It's not always about going in and selling our technology, but understanding how to solve the customer's problems, and, if you do that, everything else comes along with that. Sometimes there's not a sale attached to it and you have to think a little bit more strategically. And in our instant gratification culture, it's hard to get people to think about that.
>
> *Episode 157, June 13, 2019*

Create value with every interaction.

David Nour:

> Whether you're early in your sales career or you're a sales pro, what are you doing to create value with every interaction, with every touch? Because the reason people are not returning your calls and emails is because you or your value proposition is not a priority. . . . People prioritize their time, their effort, their resources for the relationships they perceive to be of the greatest value.
>
> *Episode 213, March 10, 2020*

One way to provide value is to share with the client what their peers are doing in the marketplace.

Dorean Kass:

> Reaching out to them and saying, "Hey, this is a terrible time, you should be working with us" is not in the spirit of the value that we add, the challenges that we solve, or our cultural values. It's much more relevant to the client to hear what their peers are doing.
>
> *Episode 220, April 10, 2020*

The value you bring to a client can be unique and creative.

Edmound Elzy leads sports and event sales teams:

> We try to build little things around it where we think we can add additional value. For example, with our suites, we allow our suite

holders to use their suites on off-days. If they want to do a meeting in a suite, we'll do that. Imagine having a good prospect that's a big soccer fan. It's a cool thing to have lunch in a suite. Maybe we can do a tour . . . That can help and be a business development tool for your company. That's the way we're trying to think about it.

Episode 383, July 23, 2021

Know in advance of a meeting what a customer's needs are and continue to be engaging over the long term.

Christopher Ware:

Before you schedule the meeting, before you send the email, already know what their needs are. At least have an idea of what that company's needs are, and then come forth with a solid solution that's going to help them overcome that obstacle and help them be more successful. If you can do that, you're going to be successful.

Episode 071, May 8, 2018

Trevor Vale:

If you're underprepared and just winging it, you're not going to extract any value from those meetings. You have to set the agenda. You have to be specific about what you want that outcome to be, the information you're looking for, and be respectful of the people you're meeting with, whether it's your colleagues or the buyers themselves.

Episode 239, June 2, 2020

Lisa Magnuson suggests "winning with themes." Read on for how she unpacks what customers truly want:

My approach to value is something called "win themes," [which is] something I've been talking about for a long time . . . The definition of win themes includes customer priorities, your strengths . . . [and] the intersection between those two things.

. . . So many times we want to share all of our strengths and have a customer try to figure out where the value is. They don't have the bandwidth for that right now. . . . You have to absolutely understand their priorities and, when I say priorities, it could be their top projects, their goals. What are their top three priorities right now

and where do those intersect with the strengths that you can bring?
... That's where the value is.

Episode 315, January 19, 2021

Your value proposition must address the challenges your customers
face today.

Maribeth Kuzmeski is the author of *And the Clients Went Wild*:

A value proposition is marketing. In marketing we've got to go for
what they want and then we can give them what they need later. But,
if we don't give them what they want, they're never going to pay any
attention ... that's why this value proposition is even more important
than ever ... it has to address what the challenges are today ...

Episode 378, June 28, 2021

Engage in deep reading to bring more value to your customers.

Mark Hunter:

What I want to focus on is, how do I create value? My whole focus
this week has been creating value for my clients and my prospects,
and I'm going to [continue to] do that by doing deep reading ... in
some journals and publications and books and so forth. It allows
me to sell with more integrity, because I can create more value. . . .

[Here's an example of what I mean.] I'm going to be an invited guest
to a board of directors meeting of a significant company. Would
they have invited me to be a participant in this board meeting if I
was seen as some schlocky? No, but clearly they see my insights as
being worth something [and deep reading informed my insights].

Episode 226, April 23, 2020

CHAPTER 15:
Bringing it All Together Like a Professional

Questions to Ponder:

- *Do you think of yourself as a Sales Professional?*
- *Are you willing to put in the time and effort to have an amazing career in sales?*
- *Do you have what it takes to get past the rejection, obstacles, and hindrances that are in your way?*

Thanks for making it through this book. I applaud you for taking the time and energy to commit yourself to a more fulfilling career in sales.

To achieve success in sales, I challenge you to think of yourself as a professional. What does that mean? What is a professional?

Think in terms of a professional athlete. They are staying healthy while also working on their mental game. They are practicing. They hire coaches. The embody a healthy lifestyle to ensure that they always have high energy and are ready to go.

You can do that. Read more books, listen to more podcasts, ask more people for advice.

I'm excited for your career success.

You made it this far.

Keep moving forward!

Acknowledgements

When I started producing the *Sales Game Changers Podcast*, I did it mainly to meet sales leaders who could join the Institute for Excellence in Sales. I didn't realize how it would change my life and impact tens of thousands of sales professionals around the globe, many who would become friends and associates.

None of this would have been possible without Deborah Ager. We had met prior to the pandemic to strategize about how to repurpose the content we were developing from the podcast. She's done an amazing job helping me clarify the content into this book and others that may come from it.

I am lucky to have two amazing parents, Joan and Herbert Diamond, three great kids (one of each), and a supportive family who have from time to time listened to the show!

There are many people who have played a role in the evolution of the podcast. Meryl Evans and Judy Schramm helped us get attention on social media. Rosario Añon Suarez was our first audio editor. Lori Saitz provided the voiceover introduction for many shows.

I knew that transcribing each episode would pay off from day one. A podcast is a living and breathing entity. It doesn't matter to me if someone listens or reads the transcript as long as they consume the content. Thanks to our talented transcriber, Mariana Badillo, for transcribing every show!

We've met some amazing people over the years at the Institute for Excellence in Sales who have helped us grow into the global organization we now run. Gina Stracuzzi has developed a world-class Women in Sales program and started hosting our weekly *Women in Sales* episode every week. John Asher, Zeev Wexler, and Tom Snyder represent the sponsors and mentors we've been fortunate to team with and learn from.

Thanks to Eaton Press for getting the book published.

Thanks to Andrea Travieso and Steven Diamond for their research on the book.

Thanks to the hundreds of guests who have appeared on the *Sales Game Changers Podcast.*

Thanks to the over one million sales professionals who have interacted with the show over the years. Congrats to you for being committed to helping customers, growing your company, and taking your career to the next level.

Index

A

Abich, Josh 35

Albright, Todd 24

Alvarez, Joe 116

Asher, John 20, 51, 108, 131, 132, 149

Atkinson, Tim 138

B

Barnes, Cynthia 30

Baron, Chris 29

Bartholomaus, Alex 70, 89

Beattie, Rob 88

Bhaskar, Vaneet 106

Bhatt, Nimit 109, 120

Bishop, Chris 28

Bjurstrom, Tonya 143

Bohannan, Nancy 31, 99

Bollini, Nick 24

Bromley, Courtney 32, 33

Brown, Doug 87

Brown, Howard 77, 139

Brown, Ryan 66

C

Cannone, Matthew 61

Cantwell, Karen 74

Cargill, Gil 60

Cerminaro, Mark 128

Cespedes, Frank 138

Cohen, Andrea 99, 133

Cook, Shawn 140

Crosbie, Jamie 110

Cutino, Chris 65, 142

D

Davison, Greg 39, 45

Donellan, Bill 52

Dorsey, Kevin 140

Dumas, Patti 100

Dunn, Bob 25

E

Egenrieder, Brian 54

Elliott Powell, Meridith 136

Elsbury, Klyn 119

Elzy, Edmound 144

F

Fisher, Jennifer 81

Franko, Amy 26, 108, 142

Freeman, GV 73

Fuentes, Will 120

G

Galvin, Karen 64, 94

Gawel, Nyla Beth 44, 45, 83

Gentry, Jane 56, 103, 104

Gilbert, Bob 114

Gonyea, Marc 95

Gordon, Gretchen 86

Green, Charles 92

H

Harman, Brian 51

Harrington, Kim 56

Hayman, Denise 72, 87

Heady, Carson 118, 125

Hecht, Michelle 133

Heiman, Alice 46, 47, 79, 108, 117

Heiman, Liz 41, 46, 95

Heiman, Stephen 46

Hendricks, Gay 96

Hunter, Mark 55, 146

I

Ives, Jennifer 33

K

Karr, Ron 37, 106

Kass, Dorean 128, 144

Kemper, Alice 26, 91

Kent, Eileen 129

Kopp, Caryn 61, 114, 126, 131

Krackeler, Chris 30, 93

Kurlan, Dave 49, 52, 59, 93, 137

Kushner, Dave 100

Kuzmeski, Maribeth 146

L

LaFleur, Mark 28

Langsam, Howard 119

Latif, Raza 28

Levine, Larry 141

Lewis, Michael 43

Ludwig, Brian 134

M

Magnuson, Lisa 145

Maier, Dan 25, 101

Maiorana, Mike 96

Markwordt, Joe 42

McDarby, Matt 48, 133

McEwen, Monica 54, 55

McGuinness, Brian 44

McKenna, Sam 69, 70

Miller, Andy 92, 109, 111, 114, 141

Milwit, Gary 13, 75, 93

Mitchell, Collin 107

Morelli, David 107

Mosley, Carrie-Anne 27, 143

Mueller, Craig 101, 135

N

Narus, Patrick 41, 42, 125
Newgaard, Gary 36, 134
Nour, David 85, 87, 123, 126, 144

P

Pepoli, Bethann 142
Peskin, Lisa 115
Poole, Deana 97, 102

R

Raheja, Pramod 129
Rakis, Angela 23
Rey, Dave 127
Richard, Steve 19, 78, 131
Riley, Melissa 124
Robbins, Anthony 139
Rodriguez, Shawn 36
Row, Shelley 50
Rowan, Bill 84
Rozenblat, Jason 32, 53

S

Salz, Lee 53, 110, 120
Savoy-Smith, Ivy 94, 127
Schijns, Janet 94, 117
Schmidtmann, Mike 60
Schramm, Judy 57, 149
Schumm, Gigi 57, 66, 71
Shanto, Tibor 98

Shen, Jeff 90

Silverman, Mark J. 34, 57

Snyder, Tom 12, 66, 149

Sobczak, Art 110

Stalmack, Adam 106

Stanley, Colleen 16, 26, 37, 69, 70, 72, 80, 102

Stein, Alan Jr 65, 89, 98, 111

Stevens, Bob 138

Su, Amy 22, 141

T

Tillma, Brynne 118

Townsend, Chris 144

Trexler, Eric 139

Turner, Caroline 143

V

Vale, Trevor 67, 145

Van Stone, Jim 88, 129

Vasquez, Javier 33, 81, 82

Via, Telesa 104

Voria, Rakhi 31, 83

W

Waltz, Andrea 29, 80, 101

Ware, Christopher 135, 145

Washko, John 82

Wexler, Zeev 130, 149

Wolinsky, Jeffrey 58

Wood, Randy 43, 130

Woodward, Christian 100

Y

Yeager, James 32
Young, Tom 135

Z

Zannetti, Gene 103
Zmuda, Christine 78

Y

Yogji, Janki 195
Young, Ben, 75

Z

Zmudzki, Jan, 195
Zulauf, Bill, 75